BEDLINGTONS
IN THE FIELD

DEDICATION

This book is dedicated to my children, Craig, Tony, Dale and Kerry, my Mam and Dad, to the memory of Ted Walsh for initially mentioning Margaret Williamson's manuscript, to Nora Williamson for sending me her mother's manuscript and finally to dearest Caroline for listening to my constant ramblings on dogs and hunting and basically for just loving me.

BEDLINGTONS
IN THE FIELD

JOHN GLOVER

Quiller

First published in the UK in 2011
by Quiller, an imprint of Quiller Publishing Ltd

British Library Cataloguing-in-Publication Data
  A catalogue record for this book
  is available from the British Library

ISBN 978 1 84689 097 0

Printed in China

Quiller

An imprint of Quiller Publishing Ltd
Wykey House, Wykey, Shrewsbury, SY4 1JA
Tel: 01939 261616 Fax: 01939 261606
E-mail: info@quillerbooks.com
Website: www.countrybooksdirect.com

CONTENTS

AUTHOR'S NOTE

It must be borne in mind that at all times it is essential to work dogs within the Law. The Law covering this is The Hunting Act 2004. If in any doubts you should seek official advice.

The author is grateful to the following for permission to use photographs in the book:

Front Cover – Rikako Fujita
Back cover – Jon Caines

Nora Williamson – 54, 55, 58, 141, 151 (*photos courtesy of*)
Dave Mills – 3, 27, 39, 49
Frances Fuller – 14, 16, 29, 39, 49, 50
Robert Penrose – 60
Ken Bounden – 36, 37, 41, 63 (*photos courtesy of*)
John Williams – 22
Laurie Fergusson – 79b
Peter Eva – 42
Sheila Smith – 74, 110, 114
Yvonne Tilbury – 156
John & Barbara Aston – 140
John Holden – 121, 161, 167
Steve Richards – 108
Caroline Englefield – 69, 100, 104, 150
Jon Caines – 79a, 168, back cover
Rikako Fujita – front cover, 1, 35, 85, 96, 98, 174
Roger Fowler – 67
Pictures by and courtesy of the Author – 21, 56, 59, 68, 76, 78, 80, 81, 86, 89, 158, 159
Matej Hraško – 44, 47, 52, 53, 95, 115, 120, 130, 136

Yours is the fell, the fen, the mountain, each green field of England's patchwork quilt. The Rat, Coney and the Tod all fall before you but above all in your chest beats the heart of a Lion in the body of the Lamb. For you are the Bedlington Terrier the gamest of the game and bettered by none.

JOHN GLOVER

PREFACE

It has never been my intention to write this book as a breed manual or a dog book in the conventional sense. At no time did I ever want this to be where you find basic dog-keeping facts or a book you delved into when the possibility of breeding a litter of pups appealed to you. This is not a book geared towards lead training, or house training or a guide into dog diseases, for these have all been covered in the past by other authors and by me.

True there are many points of historical interest, for the Bedlington terrier's past is a blood-spattered one where terriers engaged in not only conventional badger digging but also badger baiting, and there was a big difference between these two despite what some would have you believe. The game Bedlington terrier, the so-called Gypsy terrier, the dog so beloved by northern and Welsh colliers alike, would always be a dog tested in the dog fighting pit, though it seems fair to conclude some of these mains were not conducted to the almost Queensberry type rules practised by the fighters of bull-blooded stock in the English Midlands or the capital city of London itself.

The care of the working dog will be covered, both the terrier proper and its kin blood and the Bedlington-bred running dog, for nowhere is fitness of more paramount importance than in a dog that catches its prey by running it down. Sadly it is now illegal to take a hare, brown or blue, and coursing dogs and fox work with terriers are now only possible under certain circumstances. It is now known as exempted hunting and it must meet certain criteria. Time and again you will read the words 'pre ban'.

This is however a book about working dogs, hunting dogs and specifically Bedlingtons in the field. Well-being is looked at, for working dogs need to be fit; it cannot possibly be any other way. They are performance animals, canine athletes, and for a dog to perform well in this way it must be fit, very fit. This book does look at show dogs but primarily old-type show dogs not the silly imposter with cowboy chap-type furnishings on its legs – a description offered to me by a well-known show judge of many, many years' standing, which I thought was so eloquently stated, I could not have described it better myself.

Bedlingtons in the Field is a book written purely about the performance animals we hold so dear, terriers who perform effectively a pest control service against the fox (exempted hunting laws do apply here), the brown rat and the humble rabbit in the UK, badgers and foxes in certain European countries and also feral pigs, sometimes wrongly termed wild boar. Bedlington-blooded lurchers still course hares abroad, and pre ban they coped well with our own brown hare in Britain.

It is my sincere hope that this book will be the next best thing to getting out there on frosty mornings or the darkest moonless night when there is an accompanying gale, and doing what man and dog has done since our ancestors first made a partnership with the wolf. This is a partnership as old as probably man himself or damn close to it at the very least and one that some would see an end to, but should that happen it will be the death knell for not only the real Bedlington terrier but a host of other working terrier breeds as well.

We will look at show-bred Bedlingtons and discuss their suitability or otherwise as working dogs, lurchers bred as they can be from a Bedlington ancestor, hybrid Bedlington terriers which one day I hope will gain their full credibility and may be recognised as a separate splinter breed – a linty coated terrier perhaps? And the working-strain Bedlington per se. So read on with me and hopefully enjoy our journey with Bedlingtons in the field.

JOHN GLOVER 2011

Introduction

The rain started three hours ago, initially as a light shower on a wind blowing westwards from the snow fields of Eastern Europe. Winter has come early this year and for the first time in living memory England has seen snow in October and now on a bitterly cold north-easterly the rain pushes in across a cold land. For a time it pattered on the window of the cottage, lightly at first but then increasing in its rage till the spots crystallised, initially as sleet and then as snow. It is the start of a long overdue winter that all have known would come one day. As sure as the fieldfares and redwings have eyed and gobbled up the rich, red hawthorn berries, rural dwellers and hunters alike now declare 'Will be a bad 'un this year.' Neither would be wrong.

A bad day to die? There is no such thing, especially when life as rich as this has been full. Every second lived in the fast lane. A life that has seen so much more than most. A casual walk and a stretch in the sun or maybe a red rosette at a summer show might well be the pinnacle for many canines. He found her as he had left her. Curled in a ball like she was every night, peaceful and restful. Today however the little bitch is cold. She has passed on, transmuted, as the rain has transformed to snow, and now like the virgin white crystals the tears are falling.

Big men don't cry. But they do and there is no shame; men built like the proverbial brick outhouse, with hands calloused and large as shovels still weep, and folk who own working dogs are no exception especially when their dog has served them so well. As the spade breaks into the whitening land, his thoughts turn to the little dog lying in the cottage, and every spit of soil unfurls a memory. That first fox bolting cleanly, his 12 bore barking into the icy dawn with a thunderous savagery. The mink that the hounds passed by, the Bedlington refusing to yield with a nose that could not keep still. A keen sense of scent

11

that may have been gifted to her by ancestors in common with the otterhound, dogs with whom she had worked.

Each mark on her peppered muzzle tells a story. Tales of resilient foxes, encounters with fast and hard-biting rats. A dreadful tear on her shoulder made by the dreaded 'gagg', otherwise known as barbed wire. No one has told the working Bedlington not to chase rabbits. Life has been hard, a hazardous adventure for this plucky little bitch, so full of gritty determination. And with such a lovely double coat: soft, characteristic light undercoat but with much darker, wiry surface guard hairs. Almost chocolate in colour, so folk would say 'By! But that's a bonny little liver lass there.' A life rich indeed, her babes travelled the globe, or at least her babies' babes did. They worked woodchuck in New Jersey and were hybridised with running dogs in Australia where their raw, blind courage was matched to the full against the evil goring tusks of the feral swine. No! There has never been a working terrier that lived a more enchanted life than our little tyke.

He looks at her now, wrapping her in his old wax jacket, a coat in which they have enjoyed so much adventure together and with his tears melting the snow flakes on his cheeks one last time she goes again to ground, never to return. 'Rest easy moi li'l beauty. It's a peaceful fireside end fer you. Fer no finer a dog e'er drew breath.' Although our hunter is heartbroken he celebrates the life he has shared with her. No illness, just a catching up of time, and a legacy that has crossed continents that would find its roots in the very infancy of Bedlington history. No red letter champions here but her pedigree would more aptly be written in blood. Her ancestors had entered the inky black earths and citadels that had been incessantly excavated back in time by Bloody Bill Brock, the badger. In a bygone age, Bedlingtons were put to ground against the badger.

The times and hunting laws may have changed but why should the dogs? After backfilling the grave and with tears still stinging his eyes the hunter returns to the cottage. A year from now he will breed a blue and tan, a great grandson of the now buried liver warrior and the world will turn, the swallows will return and fewer cuckoos will call, but the working Bedlington will continue ... this is their story.

Yu'l ne'r do any good wastin' and spendin' yer time with them skinny slips for dogs, on the other hand yu'l ne'r go 'ungry too.

1 The Working Bedlington

So much has happened to me since I wrote my first book *The Working Bedlington* but one thing that hasn't changed is my desire to see an ideal, all-round working terrier that can still be justifiably termed the fourth of the major types of traditional working terriers. These are the fell types of terrier, the white-bodied types in several different forms, the Border terrier and of course our beloved Bedlington terrier.

A fine example of a dark working Bedlington, Plashett Mahogany owned by Frances Fuller.

Other terrier breeds have gone the way of the dodo regarding working terriers and many fine types have been lost. These include the Dandie Dinmont terrier, the Manchester, and even the dog that was once known as the Halifax blue, the Yorkshire terrier. It is fortunate that enthusiasts like Harry Parsons keep alive the working qualities of the Sealyham terrier or else they too would be another breed destined to the ranks of show terrier, for it is thanks to Parsons and his fellow enthusiasts that this breed has a great future. The Lucas and sporting Lucas terriers also have a strong working following, these two breeds or types having links to the working Sealyham which in turn I believe has a strong genetic link to Welsh valley working Bedlingtons. (The Dandie Dinmont has always been linked to the Sealyham.)

Our hunting laws, dictating how we can and cannot work terriers, have changed somewhat since my first book but the fundamentals of a real Bedlington haven't moved one iota. I still want to see good dark coats. I still want to see longer backs and I want to see high prey drive, something sadly some dogs still don't have. If we break things down we have possibly four different factions within the Bedlington breed at the moment. They are as follows:

a) The pure-bred working Bedlington terrier (both registered with the Kennel Club and not)
b) The dog owned by show fanciers who want to work and show their dogs (a very controversial point and one that will be covered at depth in a later chapter)
c) The show fancy who are only interested in showing
d) The Bedlington hybrid

It is my opinion that the show world can achieve more typical Bedlingtons by summoning up the bravery required to fly in the face of what is considered 'correct' dog politics. By using pure-bred registered working stock they can achieve far superior coats, conformation and, dare I say, prey drive or hunting instinct. Why, oh why would a show fancier want high prey drive, I hear you ask. I will tell you. They want it when they are selling puppies as capable of being working terriers. Well guess what, guys. Wouldn't it be just great if they really did or could be capable of working! Something obviously has to change radically here and I will tackle this at a later stage in the book.

The Bedlington hybrid cannot accurately be termed a working Bedlington terrier, but it can be called a Bedlington type or a Bedlington cross or, certainly, a Bedlington hybrid, also unkindly named a bastardised Bedlington, but a bastard it is. With a little thought and care though it can become a type, and a viable one at that. It can however be termed a working terrier and one I hasten to add that will work its proverbial socks off – but hybrid it is. At present. However a great potential is here for a dog thus bred, for now is the time for this dog to become standardised and thus a type or maybe a breed will be born? A working terrier that takes its roots in the Bedlington but without the constraints of the Kennel Club, allowed to more freely develop with new colours not recognised in the Bedlington per se, such as black-nosed reds, blue and red grizzle, black and chocolates.

An improved Bedlington type. Frances Fuller's Bruno.

Later I will cover Bedlington-bred lurchers, that is to say a bastardised running hound that has strong links to a Bedlington parent or perhaps grandparent. Nowhere will I call it however a greyhound or a whippet, likewise neither will I call a Bedlington × Lakeland, for example, a Bedlington as it has been in the past. I want fanciers to be honest with not only other people but with themselves too. I do hope that this is not an overambitious wish, although I am certain it will ruffle a lot of feathers.

There have been numerous occasions in the past when people have criticised me for apparently doing a U-turn on hybridising or outcrossing in the production of the working Bedlington terrier, after all I have in the past engaged in cross-breeding programmes within Bedlingtons. We will always need pure-bred sound working Bedlingtons, and by this I do mean dogs of genuine working strain rather than show dogs that do some work. So what exactly is meant by doing some work? To most working folk that usually means lots of work, day in day out, and effective performances at that. Few if any dogs are good at work if their possibilities and chances to work are few and far between. But for these dogs to be any use for either hybridising or just breeding pure-bred Bedlingtons they need to have the requisite qualities as you cannot possibly breed in good quality characteristics if they are not there in the parent dog already. Two minuses never make a plus, but then again neither does a plus and a minus make a plus either. I have lost count of how many times show fanciers have told me they have a dog that works, and one glance usually is enough to convince me 'not in this life my friend', as often the dog is so well groomed and barbered as to tell me the dog does not get anywhere near the time it would need to make even an average worker. But, don't run away with the idea that there are no working show dogs, for there are. Getting a show-bred dog to work is a relatively simple task; what cannot be done is rectifying those awful physical characteristics that are so untypically Bedlington, well a real old-fashioned one anyway.

Back to that question of some work – make no mistake the terrier that works rats and rabbits is still a working dog, very much so, especially if we remember the description of a sporting terrier as seen by one of the working terrier world's great champions, George Newcombe. George often remarked to me that a terrier was as only as good as its nose, and no truer words have ever been uttered when it comes to

17

working terriers, Bedlington or otherwise. It is a fact that there are a significant number of show-bred workers doing some work and others that don't do a single thing but their owners like to think they do. Curiously enough this is usually so when a bitch has a last pup or two in need of a home and the old sales pitch of 'work or show' comes into play. It is indeed those old characteristics, noticeable only in their absence, that make the modern show dog untypical of a real old-type Bedlington terrier. Cat feet, barrel ribs, eye set and poor coat are all encountered, and the white Bedlington is as untypical as is the pure black one often touted as a Bedlington at working terrier shows or on internet working terrier forums.

There is no doubting that the very best of the Gutchcommon dogs (Margaret Williamson's terriers) were superb in this respect, especially the dogs of the '60s and '70s, though sadly dogs bred later in my opinion started to deteriorate as they seemed to be bred closer and closer together, and constitutional unsoundness and overall frailness and eye problems all started to manifest themselves. Working terrier men didn't like that and a big shift had already started towards George Newcombe's Rillington-bred dogs and general cross-breeding or out-crossing programmes.

Newcombe's Rillingtons were regularly worked with various North Yorkshire foxhound packs, and in latter years worked with George on ferreting forays (though it should be pointed out his blue bitch Donna was a ferret killer as I sadly knew only too well for she is the only dog I have taken charge of that slew one of my fitches). There is no question that the pure Rillingtons worked and worked well, but equally their coats were nothing special and generally they were too large for most southern British hunters. George often described his dogs as viable moor dogs, and I am sure they were but there is more to Britain than just the North Yorkshire moors.

Newcombe called modern show stock 'pseudo Bedlingtons', a description apt in many instances but not all the show folk were complacent regarding the show dogs' shortcomings, especially old school breeders who were lucky enough to remember what a real Bedlington terrier looked or should look like. Ken Bounden was one such breeder. Others however were not of Bounden's ilk and one prominent breeder and exhibitor was known to have said 'if the judges won't pick my dogs I will breed a dog that at all costs they will pick.' This attitude sounded the death knell to the typical sound terrier for the judges quite simply did pick that 'pseudo Bedlington' of which Newcombe so scathingly talked and thus the biggest nail to go in the coffin of the modern Bedlington terrier was hammered down.

Roy Mee of Leicester and John Piggin of Eakring in Nottinghamshire were both great admirers of working-type dogs, especially Gutchcommon stock, though John did breed his famous bitch Lena to George Newcombe's Norman (a first-cross Lakeland/Bedlington), a union that produced two well-known blue and tans, namely Les Robinson's Amy (a huge beast of a bitch) and Newcombe's Venus, a bitch I always felt was both big and poor of coat, though to be fair Newcombe liked her. Messrs Mee and Piggin both visited Bryncock Farm, the home of Margaret Williamson, and ended up with better than average Gutchcommon stock.

Jasper of Kentene was a typical Gutchcommon-type dog but better than average – no beauty for sure but an important stud dog with a good coat who actually worked. Piggin had ample opportunity living in a remote quiet area and working as a council rodent operative. Mee, on the other hand, knew the modern Gutchcommon dogs better than anyone on the planet and inherited all of Williamson's pedigrees upon her death. Buzzer and Rex, two blue dogs, sired many litters, and many offspring of three dogs, Kentenes Rogue, Rogue of Birkacre and Piggin's Jasper of Kentene, slowly but surely started to get into diluted working-strain dogs, that is to say working-bred terriers with more than just a hint of show blood. The silly thing is it improved the show-type dogs that were owned by some working terrier folk. Now this may have came about quite by accident rather than design for it is true that a number of so-called working terrier advocates just simply thought any old Bedlington would do, as long as it didn't have a show cut on its coat and it would be possible to blag your way around any subsequent litters that may be bred from unions of dogs thus bred. By now we had a situation where working blood was entering the show lines and, guess what, the dogs in varying degrees were actually beginning to improve the general overall conformation within the modern Bedlington terrier, but just sometimes, not always!

Some show fanciers recognised this possibility and had the guts to

19

fly in the face of fashion and actually use good-coated working stock, which almost certainly meant Gutchcommon or predominantly Gutchcommon-bred stock. One lady who showed her dogs actually approached me with the intention of using a son of Jasper of Kentene. Unbeknown to us the dog was not registered with the Kennel Club and I do believe never did become registered. He had been laid off to me by Roy Mee and had known other homes before, which was a great pity for the dog was below par mentally in my opinion due to his lack of a permanent home, was bad with other dogs (certainly not desirable in any terrier least of all a Bedlington), but the real shame was he became a wasted Bedlington who could have been great if he had been fortunate enough to have had a good start in life. As it was Roddy went from pillar to post, was passed clinically unaffected by copper toxicosis, never saw a permanent working home because he was aggressive to other dogs and, in the case of our lady show breeder and others, I believe never had his pups registered simply because there was a dispute over a stud fee for the use of Piggin's dog Jasper, the sire of Roddy. John Piggin never got a stud fee from either Roy Mee or Elizabeth Curran Cooper. As I said, a great pity for his pups greatly improved the conventional show dogs, but the thing was they could not be registered with the KC. With a heavy heart our show person sold on her unregistered pups to pet homes despite possibly being the best Bedlingtons she had ever bred! This does prove a point that KC-registered working stock should be available to the show folk, for we would all like to see a situation with the Bedlington terrier similar to that of the pure-bred whippet, where the breed can still claim to be work and show dogs. Sadly, this is not the case with the Bedlington terrier.

Nevertheless, the KC should not be needlessly decried for the organisation in its rawest form is just a breed-recording service which relies totally on the honesty and integrity of the people who record and therefore register their dogs there. Me? I let Roddy go back to Roy Mee for frankly I don't tolerate aggressive dogs in the kennels and neither did I want the hassle entailed with an unregistered dog when It was used to registered stock. Roddy went back to Roy and what happened to him from there I don't know. I went away and bought a half-brother of his from John Piggin, and never looked back. That dog

Eddy Riley with The Mad Ratter.

wasn't equal to Roddy; he was better, for he kennelled well, worked great, was registered and forged a dynasty. Like Roddy that terrier was liver, and was known as The Mad Ratter.

The Mad Ratter was a sturdy dog, an absolute tiger and, back in those pre-ban days of yesteryear, worked underground to fox. Bracken was dead game, silent in his work, a mixer, he loved his underground work. He mated Robin Pickard's bitch Bess (Little Tyke of Clearwater) to produce a blue bitch also called Bess, and this bitch in turn bred a Dandie Dinmont-type dog called Stan, a dynamite liver dog who was outcrossed to a Glen of Imaal terrier. The Mad Ratter's most significant union was however probably Rock Star, a scrap of a dark blue bitch called Tina.

Rock Star was a tiny bitch, flexible and lithe as a fox, and on looks alone I took on this bitch. She had arrived from Middlesex with Reg Doyle, a lurcher and terrier enthusiast who had visited my house for a Glen of Imaal terrier. As it was Doyle left with a Glen and two pups after we had thrashed out a deal to secure his fifteen-week-old Bedlington pup he had bought from the Manchester region. I don't know why Doyle parted with her or how I convinced him, but I am just glad he did for Tina was as good a Bedlington as I ever knew despite the fact she did carry some show blood. She died when she was eighteen, toothless and blind but had lived life to the full – as vocal as The Mad Ratter had been mute, but nonetheless an efficient bolter of pre-ban foxes. Tina was an absolute joy to work, but her greatest feat was being mated to the liver dog Bracken, aka The Mad Ratter, for not only did the pair produce Rat Pit Billy, another modern working Bedlington icon but also John

Denton's Kizzy, a bitch who with further infusions of show blood produced Stuart Staley's Minkstone of Maverick, otherwise known as Rambo.

Denton's line may have followed a more direct link to the show stock, but I didn't with mine, for I directed it back to Gutchcommon stock or predominantly Gutchcommon stock. There are of course the Bedlington terrier owners who don't actually want one for work in any way, shape or form and in this we need to include both some show owners and keepers of pet animals. Despite this there is no reason why sound, typical Bedlingtons cannot be bred, after all isn't this what most owners of Bedlingtons aspire to have, a true terrier which can still work? Clearly and sadly this isn't the case in the vast majority of cases.

George Newcombe at Rillington in North Yorkshire. Newcombe pioneered modern outcrossing in Bedlingtons (photograph by John Williams).

That prominent show judge and admirer of working dogs, Stuart Yearley, has always been interested in working dogs as well as showing. John Holden is of similar ilk. In Sunderland Billy Fisher is another show enthusiast who has an interest in the working Bedlington. This is all very well but the facts remain: the modern show dog on average is still wanting in many areas, especially physical characteristics. Holden's Granitor dogs however have an awesome reputation for producing not only excellent workers but also brilliant coats. Then there is the hybrid Bedlington, produced by a practice commonly called outcrossing i.e. that is bringing in outside blood to create a working terrier. This practice was started more or less by George Newcombe, and I intend to cover this subject fully in Chapter 6.

2 A Way Forward

Within the last fifty years, Bedlingtons as working terriers have been very much viewed as a minority breed. The Bedlington however hasn't always been in the minority. In the late nineteenth and early twentieth centuries its reputation as a game, bloodstock terrier was very well known. It had already spawned the Lakeland terrier and the Border was clearly a related breed, and like its Lakeland counterpart owed some of its ancestry to the old terrier of Rothbury Forest, alias the Bedlington terrier. The true Patterdale terrier is the open-coated game wheaten, blue, chocolate (perhaps a true liver colour) and blue and tan fell terrier (also significantly brindle too). This is a star's flight away from the smooth and broken-coated red and black bull terrier-headed dogs that are erroneously referred to as Patterdale terriers today (the hard-bitten Breay/Buck-type terriers).

Old working Bedlingtons were always a popular choice for anyone engaged in a lurcher breeding project. That popularity doesn't appear to have waned, though curiously, working-strain Bedlingtons, genuine working strains, had become the minority. George Newcombe of Rillington in North Yorkshire, that doyen of the working Bedlington, believed that it was in the mid 1950s that we saw the general decline of the real old-fashioned Bedlington terrier, for by now the show fraternity had well and truly embraced the breed and in common with the show greyhound, bulldog and exhibition basset hound (amongst many other breeds) the Bedlington's fate was sealed. A show career awaited it and Newcombe had coined the expression 'pseudo Bedlington'. I couldn't have agreed with George more.

Margaret Williamson, that other great champion of the working Bedlington, was also of the opinion that the modern show dog had deteriorated considerably and that the Bedlington had become a shadow of its former self. Indeed Williamson's terriers were greatly prized for their type and specifically for their superb coat. Today we often see dogs reputedly of this breeding with appalling soft colourless coats, and it must be stressed that these animals are NOT typical Gutchcommons. Both Rillington (George Newcombe) and Gutchcommon (Margaret Williamson) can be regarded as working strains.

Other enthusiasts also embraced the cause of the working Bedlington, and they included Nigel Evans, Dave Roberts, John Piggin, Roy Mee and me, all of us old school enthusiasts who remembered and worked (and still do) typical working Bedlingtons. Indeed it was Dave Roberts who may have provided the nearest answer to a third working strain with his Garthforest line of terrier. In the light of how Newcombe's dogs were bred I would say that was almost a racing certainty. Newcombe was of the same opinion.

John Piggin and I had dogs with Gutchcommon breeding and diluted show breeding. We inherited that breeding from terriers bred into the working stock, undesirable certainly, however it did prove that modern show breeding could be bred out with selection. This is a point that I feel show people should look at and have the resolve to use these dogs. These animals would dramatically improve their terrier's type in a very short space of time. In point of fact one of the most promoted and well-known of working Bedlingtons carried some show breeding, yet the dog was anything but show type, proof if ever I needed it that show blood and type can be quite easily bred out. Again show breeders should look at this and decide if they want to see a return to the glory days of the early twentieth century when the breed could justly claim to be 'work and show'. Stuart Staley's Minkstone of Maverick (aka Rambo) was one such dog; no one could have ever denied that Rambo was a typical working Bedlington that definitely worked pre ban to ground on fox.

A situation now sadly exists where too many three-minute wonder enthusiasts come into the breed, work a rat or rabbit and then say they have a working Bedlington. New laws or not, one should remember there is a way that a fox can still be worked legally (exempted hunting); the breed did not forge its reputation as one of the gamest terriers to ever draw breath just by killing rats or chasing rabbits. We all know it's fun, but it is not serious work.

The late Roy Mee kept out and out Gutchcommon-bred Bedlingtons, but just how much Roy worked his dogs I don't honestly know. I knew Roy very well but never went out in the field with him. That said, Roy Mee did advocate using and breeding working stock, and he also knew Margaret Williamson extremely well and knew her strain inside out. George Newcombe, as controversial as ever, had voiced the opinion that in order for him to continue with his strain of terrier it may be advantageous to outcross (cross-breed) into the line rather than use either show breeding or Gutchcommon strain (it was well known that the latter were disliked by Newcombe), though he had previously used the breeding and latterly did so with John Piggin's Lady Lena of Eakring. George subsequently crossed in both pedigree Lakeland terriers and unregistered fell terriers, and in latter years Newcombe also experimented with a Border terrier outcross.

He was not alone with outcrossing either. Several enthusiasts also set about similar projects. I myself set up two hybrid lines although one of these was to breed a Dandie Dinmont-type terrier. Subsequently many working terrier enthusiasts adopted the outcrossing policy and whilst some stick to the basic Lakeland cross others set about using black fell terrier breeding which may or may not have carried white-bodied terrier blood. With this, variance started to creep in and whilst we could never have described the dogs as show Bedlingtons, we could equally never call them working-strain Bedlingtons. In fact some could have justified the title mongrel terriers for a situation now exists where some hybrids are the result of being produced from two different outcross breeds, for example both Lakeland and maybe black fell terrier appear.

Let me state this here and now. First-cross hybrid Bedlingtons can and do make excellent working terriers, but they are just that – hybrids (until the day comes along, in the not too distant future, when a new type manifests itself). As one-offs they can be superb, but by the time a second cross is used back to the Bedlington the end result can be nothing short of horrendous, for in many instances we are back to poor coats and curiously outlandish large terriers are sometimes produced. This happened when John Piggin used George Newcombe's Norman (a first-cross Lakeland × Bedlington) to his blue bitch Lena (as has just been explained). One of these pups, Les Robinson's Amy, was quite large though I do gather Les bred some useful lurcher types from out of this bitch. (Incidentally, according to reports, Les Robinson also wrote under the pseudonym N. Bird.)

Bedlingtons are used for lure coursing in the USA.

Personally I still think the Bedlington can be saved within the confines of the breed (these animals may prove beneficial to outcrossing programmes too), not that this task will be an easy one either, however by careful selection and using constitutionally sound stock I do firmly believe this is possible. The biggest problem is a small gene pool.

Taking this on apace, I feel this is good for anyone who works, breeds or requires a genuine Bedlington lurcher. Given the choice, most lurchermen want to use pure-bred stud dogs, and the generally accepted way is when a Bedlington dog is paired to a greyhound bitch. But I feel I should give the reader this point to ponder. Would the vast majority want a lurcher thus bred (Bedlington sire to greyhound dam), or a Bedlington × Bedlington/Lakeland × whippet/greyhound? Both are fifty per cent running dog and fifty per cent terrier but only one is a genuine F1 or first-cross hybrid. I believe I know what most running dog enthusiasts would choose, and I know which one I would want, if only to simplify matters and know what you have got! There is no

27

denying that one of the primary reasons there has been a big resurgence of interest in the working Bedlington is the fascination the breed gets from owners of lurchers. Actually it was the first thing that lured me to the breed, and the obsession developed from there.

I am sure we have all met from time to time dishonest breeders of lurchers and terriers, the type of person who sells a litter of deerhound × greyhound longdogs one week and offers the remaining puppies as Bedlington × greyhounds a fortnight later. The strange thing is that some of these sellers actually gain respect for some silly reason. This type of scenario can be found regarding certain litters of Bedlingtons, which brings me to a story.

Several years ago I was 'kindly' offered an opportunity to buy a 'well bred working Bedlington pup, off working stock', from a seller who did have a reputation for breeding lots of pups, both running dogs and terriers, and claimed to be descended from some mythical Gypsy tribe who lived totally upon their wits, scrap metal, peg making and owning the best hunting dogs on Mother Earth. Well there I was with a gullible punter who wished to mate his collie lurcher to whatever running type our vendor invented on any given day, and it could be anything – honest! You wanted it, and it was there – back to the Bedlingtons!

My companion comments, 'John keeps Bedlingtons.' The vendor says 'I have a litter of Beddys,' (I deplore that description – it's Bedlington terrier!) 'ave a look, hey mate, buy one if yer want.' I didn't but that was by the by. Let's have a jolly old look! Well there were our terriers both doing their best Bob Marley impressions with accompanying dreadlocks of matted coats (always a bad sign) and an enthusiastic seller telling me how these were 'proper working Bedlingtons', and 'not yer show shit!' 'Do you have the dogs' pedigrees?' I asked. One glance was enough to convince me they were total show stock, and furthermore both the dogs had been given to him by someone who in turn had picked them up for free. This was obvious deception. The thing was I knew the show person who had given the dogs away initially, and this obviously should not have happened, because an initial agreement had been made that if the dogs were let go they went back to their original owner.

The end result was one very upset show person for being led up the proverbial garden path, an offended vendor when I told him he should not sell show stock as genuine working stock, and in all probability yet more inferior stock going on the market as working-strain Bedlingtons! Such actions do nothing for the cause of the real working Bedlington. (Thinking about it neither does the pretend hunting element we currently have in so-called working Bedlingtons but that again is another matter!)

Bedlington terriers and lurchers often go hand in hand. It is the romantic vision of horse-drawn Gypsy caravans, camp fires, and tripods holding bubbling cauldrons of delicious game stew that spring to mind. Within these mythical camps would be lamb-like dogs and blue/black

A good-headed working Bedlington belonging to Frances Fuller.

rough-coated greyhounds (Bedlington lurchers), dogs that will sneak off in the first light to deliver a rabbit breakfast for their waking owner a couple of hours later. It's a quaint vision but in reality it's about as likely as hell freezing over.

Even so it is this very vision that attracts enthusiasts to the Bedlington terrier. Terriers shown in the early part of the twentieth century were very different from today's bench winners, and even immediate post-war Bedlingtons were a far cry from today's show bench red letter champion. Such dogs were typical of a real Bedlington: dark, yes; black, no; liver and true sandy, yes; the chocolate of a Labrador, no; and off-white, definitely not. The true colouration of the real Bedlington also seems to have been largely lost in recent years. Yes, those original dogs were dark, but they did carry an almost white top knot which was very silky to the touch, they had light braiding on their legs, their coats were of a true hard lint, double coated and a star's flight away from today's modern show dog. Some of Frances Fuller's dogs are of this ilk.

There is also scant reference to black-nosed red dogs and blue grizzles, both colours found in Border terriers, a related breed. It is here that the hybrid enthusiasts could really make their mark by endeavouring to breed a type of terrier, but not necessarily calling it a Bedlington, but a Bedlington type. It could not be a Rothbury, for that has already been done and in fact it is a Bedlington, but a linty coated terrier isn't. Brian Plummer did something similar with his Plummer terrier, which is Jack Russell-like but not a Jack Russell, and the same was true with the sporting Lucas terrier as opposed to the Lucas terrier. (I shall discuss this in depth in my chapter on outcrossing.)

One of the biggest problems facing the working Bedlington is a limited gene pool; in reality all that is left is Gutchcommon or part-bred Gutchcommon (that is to say Gutchcommon stock watered down with modern show stock, and here John Piggin's Lena and Floyd spring to mind). Only clever line breeding can keep this type of terrier sound and it can be done by mating only sound working terriers together that do not manifest physical problems or faults, such as, at worst, weedy specimens with weak bottom jaws and eye problems including cataracts – only the soundest to sound I am afraid, and this was certainly the case when I used John Piggin's liver dog Floyd of Eakring, for Floyd's offspring and their offspring were incredibly balanced terriers that worked and had that typical Bedlington temperament of old, a do-or-die nature so beloved by northern and Welsh hunters in particular.

Rillington-bred dogs of course did offer an alternative, though to be fair the pure-bred Rillington had gone a long time ago, at least one that had not been hybridised. Recently there has been a lot of promotion and excellent reports regarding John Holden's Granitor-bred dogs that are used in working circles, and this is something we shall look at in the chapter on the working show dog. Whichever way we care to look at it, the working Bedlington, its hybrid brethren, and its lurcher offspring are immensely popular. Nowadays few country shows or fairs don't have at least a handful of Bedlingtons in attendance and in the case of some shows, The Heart of Wales in particular, Bedlingtons seem to be very well catered for.

In Britain where the hunting laws have changed in recent years we have a scenario where dogs are subjected to exempted hunting (to be discussed in my chapter on the law) and rat and rabbit hunting. The fact that both of those quarry species are on the increase indicates that the popularity of both Bedlington and the Bedlington-bred lurcher are set to continue. Only very recently I witnessed a show-bred dog working cover and it was efficient and thorough in its hunting. There was a Granitor-bred dog there as well alongside a hybrid that contained show as well as Lakeland terrier breeding. Show-bred dogs will work but they can be vastly improved on. Out should go the rounded ribs, poor coats and short camel or roached backs. Getting a show dog to work is one thing (easy as it goes) but it won't correct those physical faults that will undoubtedly make a difference when the chips are really down on a hard day's work.

Jack Walker of Shepshed had a wonderful bitch that came from I believe the Whetstone breeder Roy Mee, a model working Bedlington bitch. Jack not only worked her on a variety of quarry but showed her at a few country shows. I gave that bitch Best Working Bedlington Terrier at a show in Bedworth, Warwickshire one cold day in November despite the fact the dog in question was undershot in the jaw. That blue bitch was typical of a real working-type Bedlington terrier, small but not weedy, with a lovely double coat of hard lint with a good colour.

A superb example of an outcrossed dog.

There is a way forward for the working Bedlington, each and every faction: the working strain, the show stock and the hybrids; indeed contrary to what some may think I predict a very positive future for hybrid dogs, what I won't do is call them Bedlingtons or Rothbury terriers but I do think there is a place for a Bedlington offshoot called possibly the linty coated terrier.

Show dogs can benefit from the pure-bred working-strain dogs as can the hybrids – a lurcher bred from a Gutchcommon Bedlington is a working running dog to behold (Gary Taylor's Bullet and Tod spring to mind). The legacy Mrs Margaret Williamson left may well be one that will be truly significant in the way forward for the real Bedlington terrier.

3 The Show Bedlington

The modern-day show Bedlington is a mere shadow of its counterpart of the immediate post-war years, of that there is no doubt. The new type was instantly recognisable as a dog too short in the back, its ribs were rounded, the coat absolutely appalling and tight cat feet had taken over from the classic Bedlington long hare foot. Puppies were being born with lots of white on them, not only nails and toes but sometimes a majority of leg, and tremendously large white blazes on breasts, and all this blended easily into a dog that eventually became to all intents and purposes 'white'. Livers were distinguished from blue specimens purely by colour of nose and nail colours, though in the case of the really poor dogs this was difficult as all the nails could be white. White colouring is out of keeping with the classic north of England/Scottish borderland working terriers. For the first time in its history (post war) the word poodle cropped up alongside the Bedlington terrier.

After the Second World War normality returned, dog showing once again commenced and the Bedlington's popularity as a show dog once again started to increase. It was this period that saw the emergence of the two major working strains of Bedlington terrier, although the dogs of the Misses Maunsell and Hamilton had always been dogs capable of both working and showing. Both of these women were judges as was Mrs Margaret Williamson whose strain was in part bred down from Maunsell's and Hamilton's dogs. Where these two strains went (into a purely working terrier world) was really down to both the attitudes of the show judges at the time (and now as it so goes) plus a dangerous shift by breeders and exhibitors to breed to win at all costs. This happened, so untypical terriers started to emerge and, horror of horrors, they started to win well. Show breeders only wanted to use the current red letter champions, but these dogs were out of keeping with the show bench winners from the early part of the twentieth century. The rot had set in – untypical was mated to untypical.

The description of the jacket as a soft linty coat opened up avenues to be exploited by the folk who wanted to win. Where did hard lint go or maybe rough, though that description probably disappeared with Ainsley's Phoebe and Piper? Goat coated was uttered with almost disgust, a derogatory description given to a terrier that was more true to type, but in fact it was a true Bedlington coat! Ken Bounden, that doyen of the breed and show judge of exceptional notability, argues that the Gutchcommon strain of Bedlington is show bred, and, yes, there is truth in this, for the Gutchcommon strain was bred from show stock, show stock that worked, show stock that was typical, show stock with real blue/black coats and true livers, non fading bi-colours (meaning liver, blue and sandy and tan) and true sandys, a recognised colour which was the colour of sea sand not at all the colour of washed-out liver (old-type show dogs, work, pet or show dogs).

Now we hear talk of Japanese, American, Australian and Swedish enthusiasts wanting 'white' Bedlingtons, asking for this colour specifically, and American show owners exhibiting dogs with furnishings so profuse that they resemble cowboy chaps on the dogs' legs – and they worry about having a hare foot! Why worry at all when the foot is not visible? I worry for the state of the modern show Bedlington for a new generation has emerged, immersed in a notion that the dog is effeminate, a toy to be pampered and preened and dressed up in fancy dress. This seriously worries me, for the dog is a northern working terrier not a doll. I genuinely feel these people do care deep down inside but are misguided, misinformed and generally live in a world where it's fitting for a woman to be called a dog's mummy and a man to be called its daddy; it's gone wrong somewhere!

Let me give an example, a parallel for you to ponder. The Italian greyhound was once a true all-purpose diminutive sight hound, capable of knocking down a rabbit in full flight, a dog fleet of foot and nimble enough to work, a genuine miniature 'whippet' if you like. Now it has been reduced to a brainless, scatty nervous little beast, out of place and out of touch with its roots, lost in a show-orientated world. Another example is the English toy terrier, the original ladies' lap dog but the darling of the rat pits, which would be galvanised into action and slay rats back in Victorian England, but which would be hard pressed to crunch a bone nowadays. Enthusiasts of both these breeds will tell you these dogs can still work, but I will tell you now that's rubbish. And in any case, is that what we want for the Bedlington terrier? For that is what will happen, but the good news is that it's not too late to stop the rot.

At a recent Bedlington Terrier Association event I was asked to judge the show dogs there that day to give my encouragement, appraisal and otherwise on the dogs there. Never would I say to some-one you must work your terrier for that is just not true; no one has the right to dictate to anyone what they must and must not do and it's not everyone who wants to work a dog. Though it's amazing how many people become working experts overnight when they have a litter of

Head study of a modern working Bedlington with show breeding. Owned by Matej Hraško.

puppies available for sale. Suddenly we have that old chestnut again 'work and show'. Yes you will get a show dog to work but what you will not do is correct the physical faults and these faults will get bigger and more acute if something is not done fast.

A genuine working-type dog, with the classic dark coat, hare foot, lighter legs, almost white top knot, with a lovely flat rib, natural rise to the loins and a long back, with good jaws and massive teeth is the ideal. Once these were show dogs, show dogs that did work. Ken Bounden remembers the type, John Holden has enough courage to pick such dogs when judging and Frances Fuller breeds such a dog (as does Lesley Caines of the Midland Bedlington Terrier Club).

Stuart Yearley of Lowbrook Bedlington Terriers also fits into this category. Margaret Williamson was a show judge of great note but she ceased showing when she realised that the show dog was going the wrong way, and a similar thing happened with George Newcombe of Rillington.

The 1950s saw a big shift in the world of the show Bedlington with many of the new type coming to the fore and once more I place the blame squarely on the shoulders of the show judges. If they had not

'Sperkeforde Jackanapes' is the yard-stick for all physically correct Bedlingtons.

Champion Brambledene Buccaneer. Nicely balanced, perfect symmetry.

picked them then the breed would not have systematically suffered. So where do we go from here? Do the show fancy sit still and let the rot go further for eventually it will and be accepted as the norm? (In fact it probably is already!) Bedlington terriers are essentially working terriers, their very heritage lies here. The breed is not a poodle, it's not a comical dog to be degraded by being dressed up in fancy dress; it is just that – a working terrier. Sperkeforde Jackanapes epitomised a real Bedlington terrier, a show dog that was typical, not only that but a working-type Bedlington terrier.

The future of the show Bedlington terrier lies within the hands of breeders like Lesley Caines, Frances Fuller and John Holden if the dog can ever be termed once again 'work and show'. That was the case many years ago, very much 'work and show'. Those who state that the Gutch-common strain of Bedlington was show bred and not a unique working strain do have an element of truth, but what they must also admit to is those early Gutchcommon 'show' dogs were of a vastly different type from that seen today. The same could have been said of the Misses Maunsell and Hamilton amongst several others too. Margaret Williamson and the Misses Maunsell and Hamilton were both judges and exhibitors of Bedlingtons. The dogs they favoured were typical earth dogs, bred along lines that were totally geared up for performance dogs.

It is interesting to hear Margaret Williamson's 'Points of the Bedlington' from a manuscript she was writing for a book that never saw publication. I was kindly given the manuscript by Margaret Williamson's daughter Nora; the book was intended to be called *The Bedlington Terrier* (later Ken Bounden had a book published by the same name).

I now quote from that manuscript, for it would be a tragedy indeed for the Bedlington terrier if some of Margaret Williamson's words never reached the masses around the globe. Margaret spoke of 'points of the Bedlington':

What are the reasons for the characteristic points of the Bedlington? Let us examine them one by one and really how clever were these Rothbury gypsies and also we must follow their lines when breeding and training workers today.

First coat – it must be weather resistant and this means a somewhat soft under coat with a profusion of stiff twisty hairs running through it which throw off the water and allow the under coat to stay dry.

Now conformation – we will start from the feet up. Feet should be hare shaped with two long toes. These enable the dog to loosen the soil as it digs and also the same shaped feet enable it to run swiftly without getting sore pads.

The hind quarters – should be rounded and muscled up, with legs closer together at foot than at hocks. The action should be a 'rolling' gait and when at speed hind feet should come up and outside the front ones, the body looking now bow shaped from the side. Incidentally, when lying down, a Bedlington will lie with his hind legs spread flat behind him, really lying on his belly.

Ribs – these should be completely flat, but the brisket should be deep allowing plenty of lung space. The body should be well coupled up and neat in appearance.

Again the front legs should be wider at shoulder than at foot, slightly shorter than the hind legs. This helps to give the typical roach appearance. Unfortunately, show enthusiasts attempt to teach the dog to stand with arched back. This false arch is really over the kidneys and a dog trying to use it in an earth would soon ruin its kidneys.

The true roach is further forward and since the dog usually digs lying on its side, the roach is of real help when digging bringing the full weight of the body behind the digging legs.

The Bedlington has two strong physical qualities, speed and power. Power to dig fast and deeply, speed to overtake a rabbit or nip a rat at the right moment.

The shoulder, therefore, should have an angle of 45 degrees and the neck be long and flexible.

Finally, the head, the very characteristic Bedlington head with a long straight jaw, large powerful teeth, ears lying flat to the cheeks and small deep set triangular eye.

The ear setting is typical, being almost in line with the jaw. The ears themselves should not be too small but should lie flat to the cheeks. Such ears are not likely to take a lot of punishment.

The deep set eyes are safe when in dense cover, sleepy looking when the dog is at rest but very sharp and alert at the least sound.

A pacey liver Bedlington from the USA.

As anyone can see this description by Margaret Williamson epitomises a typical Bedlington terrier and dogs thus bred would truly be both work and show. Margaret Williamson credited the Gypsies of the Rothbury Forest area as being the earliest keepers of prototype Bedlingtons, in a time when in all probability the dogs were called simply 'terriers'. She credits the original name as Rothbury terrier, then the Pitmans terrier before 1825 when Ainsley's Piper was born and went on to be known as the first Bedlington terrier. Margaret Williamson maintained absolutely that there were two very distinct types of post-war dogs, and these are and were the show and working types. 'This was doubtless due to Poodle crossing allowed by the Kennel Club.' Margaret Williamson was a Bedlington enthusiast through and through, owning Bedlington terriers since 1904 and first exhibiting her dogs in 1921. In her latter years she kept up to twenty-two Bedlingtons which she bred only for working.

Ken Bounden in *The Sporting Bedlington*, which was the official newsheet of The National Bedlington Terrier Club, in February 1968 about the time he visited Margaret Williamson, wrote: 'If what I saw in Wales is any indication of the potential then I must argue that better coats would be more common if we made use of the Valley dogs.' Margaret Williamson and George Newcombe had both been involved with showing but deplored what had happened to the breed and, whilst at a later date the two great stalwarts of the working Bedlington would disagree and a split would divide them, The Working Bedlington Terrier Club for a time at least united as these two led the campaign for typical working-type Bedlington terriers, and they agreed wholeheartedly on one thing in particular – in a word, poodle!

Williamson writing in *Shooting Times & Country Magazine* makes mention of a previously published work in the same magazine where Frank Warner Hill wrote: 'definitely stated that the Kennel Club approved a crossing of a "crisp coated miniature poodle with a Bedlington". Following this cross, I feel sure that the present woolly coat has been accepted by the showing fraternity as it is easier to trim and also hides faults of conformation. Unfortunately, it has almost destroyed the true Bedlington type and produced a coat totally unfit for work.' The biggest problem today is as it was back in the 1960s and '70s. The show people generally shun working Bedlingtons and the working faction quite simply deplore the dogs they called 'mincing fluffys'. One difference back then was that there were two cups at a National Bedlington Terrier Club show, each trophy taking its name from two of Margaret Williamson's well-known terriers – Musha and Worton Demon. The late John Piggin, the Newark rat catcher, won both of these trophies with his dogs; the Musha Challenge Cup was for the best working bitch and the Worton Demon Challenge Cup for the best dog.

So what is the hope for a return to the days when dogs worked and still became show bench champions? Bedlingtons like Norman Stead's Champion Spring Dancer, Cranley Blue Boy or maybe Sudston Miner, a beautifully balanced and powerfully built Bedlington from 1915. Or the three incredible Bedlingtons: Ulsterman, Princess and Champion Breakwater Pierette.

The National Bedlington Terrier Club was established a long time ago, in 1875, and the club has seen the glory days when Bedlingtons were champions because they were typical, real dogs. Would Sudston Miner, that superb dog I just mentioned of 1915, get a look in today? I very much doubt it.

The dogs have changed massively since Joseph Ainsley produced Young Piper in 1825. This was the first Bedlington terrier by name but not the best by any stretch of the imagination, for by the year 1844 T.J. Pickett had bred the celebrated and beautiful Tyneside. The

Norman Stead's Champion Spring Dancer. A show dog that worked regularly to fox.

41

Bedlington terrier systematically suffered at the hands of the show fancy; true some dogs worked but all the same the breed started on its slippery downward spiral. By the mid-twentieth century Fred Gent's Foggyfurze Bedlingtons were clearing up at KC shows and by the 1970s and '80s Stanolly stock was a popular show line. The untypical, rather than typical terriers had taken precedence. To be fair Ken Bounden of Exeter, Devon was very critical of the show dogs, for not only was the type poor in several differing points but copper toxicosis and various eye problems were causing major problems within the breed (see my book *The Working Bedlington*).

Lowbrook Laurel. Stuart Yearley's blue show and working dog (photograph Peter Eva).

Newcombe and Williamson both were increasingly aware of the overall deterioration of the Bedlington and that basically marked the change. Historically, the Gutchcommon strain may well have been the last of the real old-type Bedlingtons for George Newcombe's dogs really had their roots in more recent show breeding, hence their overall height and not so good coats. It is encouraging to see breeders such as John Holden, Frances Fuller and Lesley Caines striving to keep, breed and promote better Bedlingtons. Stuart Yearley, a Londoner by birth but countryman at heart, keeps, exhibits and judges Bedlingtons. Like Holden, Fuller and Caines he is also an advocate of more typical Bedlingtons.

From Pickett's Tyneside to the modern show lines of Foggyfurze and Stanolly may seem a long time, but the dog show had got its grip and like a bulldog with a bone it was not going to let go. Wars came and went but showing just as surely came back again and again. The untypical became the accepted but for two lines: Gutchcommon and Rillington.

4 The Working Show Dog

Do show dogs work? Can they work? The answer is yes! Now comes the snag: whilst you can get a show dog to work what you cannot do is rectify physical faults, untypical characteristics that are not in keeping with a real Bedlington terrier. Show dogs get worked, or rather they do some work, which usually means working above ground to rabbit and rat, or being used in a gun dog's role. This is all very commendable, but the real Bedlington terrier did work, and pre ban that included underground work to fox, and in a bygone age badger and otter too.

Show-bred worker in Slovakia.

When the show judges of the post-war period decided in their infinite wisdom to pick an untypical dog the show fanciers had a choice to breed this untypical dog and win, or carry on with a typical work and show dog and quite frankly not win. Sadly some took the former route, and for the Bedlington terrier, or *real* Bedlington terrier it sounded a potential death knell.

OK, we had a situation where untypical dogs with poor fronts, camel backs, rounded ribs and tight cat feet were winning, and the word 'poodle' was mentioned but was denied totally. The fact is the modern-day show dog is very poodle-like in appearance, where a real Bedlington most certainly is not. Not all show judges picked or even liked that modern show dog; indeed some were very critical including such eminent judges as Ken Bounden, John Holden and Stuart Yearley.

A good number of show Bedlingtons were pet dogs that just occasionally got bred from, and with the increasing popularity of working Bedlingtons such animals were sought by hunters, especially when certain specimens became available and were advertised locally. Pups from such litters, untypical though they may be, were being termed working Bedlingtons. There were some decent trainers who had these dogs and worked them with a certain degree of success and whilst the dogs went on to be called working Bedlingtons they did not fully represent a real working, or old-fashioned working Bedlington.

So what is a working Bedlington, a real working Bedlington? Sadly to a lot of folk that means a Bedlington that does *any* work and that simply is not true. Both the late Margaret Williamson and George Newcombe abhorred the modern show dog and their reaction was to shun them and walk away from the world of show Bedlingtons. Despite this some folk were working show-bred dogs, and indeed both Stanolly and Foggyfurze dogs have been used in the hunting field. These families of Bedlingtons are in fact the two main show lines, and it follows that terriers bred from these strains have been worked. Abroad where showing is of course very popular, especially in northern Europe, certain show-bred dogs have been tried on a variety of heavy and sometimes toothy quarry.

In Britain our laws have changed dramatically regarding what we can and cannot catch, and now you are a criminal if your dog catches a hare but you can fly a bird of prey on the same animal. Similarly, there are ways around hunting fox to ground under exempt hunting laws, although generally the lot of a fox hunter is not good in Britain at the time of writing. As Britain and Eire is the traditional home of all working terriers it is indeed a tragedy that the laws in the UK now restrict the use of its terriers. The rest of the world looked upon our islands as the premier producer of top working terriers and as such our valiant working breeds have travelled across continents. The Americans, on the other hand, are quite flexible regarding the use of working terriers, especially in their earth dog trials where a variety of terriers are used including not only the Bedlington but also to a lesser extent breeds such as Welsh, West Highland white and Cairn terriers. Gradually the working terrier has been stifled and this started long before the current hunting restrictions with dogs came into force.

So what are those traditional quarry species? Traditionally it was mainly foxes and badgers, but also otter, mink, rats and rabbits. Fox hunting is now restricted on what can be practised legally, whilst the badger was gradually phased out and eventually forbidden as a quarry species. The otter was eventually banned altogether (like the badger) when it was decreed that the species was endangered, and restrictions were also applied to mink, hare and grey squirrels. Only the rat and the humble rabbit remained unrestricted as quarry species. Even the pesky house mouse was afforded some protection from the hunting with dogs laws!

The rest of the world of course had different laws and in countries where badger digging was allowed working terriers including the Bedlington terrier worked the badger underground. Fox worked continued unhindered and working terriers thrive outside of their native homelands of Britain and Eire. At this point I think it is only fair to point out that there always was a big difference between badger digging and badger baiting, just as there is a massive difference between rat hunting with terriers and rat baiting (the rat pits of Victorian England illustrate this last point perfectly). Badger digging when conducted properly did serve a humane and effective form of control when brock was deemed a pest. At the end of a badger dig the animal was humanely dispatched or taken from the sett and let loose at another location; all this is now illegal of course including the liberation of the animal.

Badger-hunting terriers were of two types: the bayer who rarely

Continental badger hunting. In some parts of Europe badger digging is still legal.

sustained injury or if it did very little, and the dead game and hard terriers that often lost teeth, or sustained broken jaws and terrible throat wounds. The badger is a wonderfully powerful fighter underground and terriers frequently died underground or afterwards from their subterranean battles. In countries where hunting the badger is legal and therefore practised, hunters still use Bedlington terriers, and, would you believe, that invariably means show-bred Bedlingtons.

Pictures sent to me of show-bred Bedlingtons with foxes show that they are utterly game terriers but not in show trim, and generally their coats are appalling. That said these terriers do see work underground, but they will be fit and may or may not be hybridised with other working terriers. I have pictures sent to me from Slovakia of show-bred dogs really mixing it with foxes – you cannot deny these dogs are game.

So what are the odds, why the big difference between working and show strain? Let's break it down and explain. The average show-bred Bedlington terrier, owned as a pet or by a show owner, will be in a majority of cases in my opinion not as fit as it could be. I recently judged a one-off class at a Bedlington Terrier Association function where the general idea was to illustrate to the majority (that means the show and pet fraternity) just exactly what we should be looking for in an ideal working Bedlington. I had quite a few entrants to judge, most of course being show dogs whose owners actually did have the courage to let me examine their dogs, though I thought it a pity that the most ideal little specimen there that day did not get entered for it looked at face value to be the best dog there.

Nevertheless I had my entrants there, including cross-breds for some bizarre reason (meaning a mongrel and a lurcher as opposed to a Bedlington hybrid). My main purpose was to illustrate where the average show-bred dog fell short. In most cases it was fitness! OK, there are physical faults not in keeping with a real Bedlington that can't be rectified, such as gun barrel fronts, camel backs or bad coats, but fitness can be achieved and more especially maintained.

At working terrier shows where Bedlingtons are catered for a vast majority will be show dogs, and both show and pet breeders will sell you a puppy for work. Even a lot of the hybrids will be bred down from show stock (George Newcombe's Venus was one such dog for she had modern show breeding and in my opinion the poor coat that goes with that, though to be fair she also had Rillington breeding). Happily there are some show judges and enthusiasts who are very critical of the average modern show-bred dog, and I include people such as Frances Fuller, John Holden and Stuart Yearley. Lesley Caines also breeds and likes a darker dog; in fact I have in front of me pictures of a dog bred by Lesley that is used in the USA for lure coursing. The picture depicts a beautifully balanced and long-backed specimen, obviously fit and in full flight. But some of the dogs I examined at Brailles in Oxfordshire at the BTA event were so unfit that a canter would be difficult for them, this despite the sterling work put in by Billy Fisher of Sunderland who does a great job at encouraging owners in terrier racing, thereby improving physical fitness. Generally speaking a working home will give a dog a fitter life, for working dogs

An American Bedlington opens up.

like all athletes, human or animal, need to be fit to perform properly.

I have judged show-bred Bedlingtons at working terrier shows, the self same type of dogs I judged for the show fraternity, and significantly the working show dogs were not only more easily spannable but their overall fitness was much, much better. The fronts were still the same, the roached backs and poor coats still evident, but what they did possess overall was a good or at least a better degree of fitness.

So what good points did I find with the show dogs? Unfortunately the best dog was not exhibited on the day for its coat was very good, its overall conformation nice and it was the correct size for underground work. We should never lose sight of the fact Bedlingtons are terriers and were designed (despite what some would have you believe) to go to ground. I was pleasantly surprised by the large teeth on some of the dogs. Stuart Yearley, a Londoner by birth but an avid admirer of working dogs, has an albeit large dog that has seen work above ground that has teeth on it that would compare to those of a bull mastiff! Indeed Stuart has used his terriers above ground in the gun dog role working both rats and rabbits.

A blue and tan Bedlington.

Several years ago in pre-ban days, I knew of a hunter from Chester who used a Stanolly-bred Bedlington to ground, and despite the fact the dog had a rubbish coat it was a good fox bitch. John Holden's Granitor dogs also carry a reputation as working dogs plus they are very dark as are Frances Fuller's dogs; both these enthusiasts strive to breed a better Bedlington and that can only be applauded.

I had a blue/black Bedlington called Rock Star that was around three parts Foggyfurze bred (show stock). Tina was a quarter working bred but no finer working terrier ever drew breath than this dog. The bitch lived until she was eighteen years of age and pre ban bolted and dug fox. She never sustained any serious injury and was paired to the Gutchcommon dog, The Mad Ratter. Not only did this union produce Rat Pit Billy, the sire of my hard-bitten blue dog Ninja, but also John Denton's Kizzy, a dog that in turn was bred to a show-bred dog, and that union produced Stuart Staley's Rambo.

Rambo is generally recognised as one of the best working Bedlington terriers in recent years yet he carried a lot of show breeding, proof if ever I needed it just how far a little, typical working breeding can go. Rambo (Minkstone Maverick) saw a lot of work underground and although I never saw him work in the flesh I did see a video of him working, and there was no denying Rambo was a great worker and a credit to his owner, Stuart Staley.

I recently saw a rather elderly show-bred dog working rough cover, working with ferrets, steady with poultry and marking rats, possibly the fastest Bedlington I have ever seen. Its owner keeps it very fit and generally overall I think it is one of the best show-bred dogs I have ever seen. Show-bred Bedlington terriers will work and do work, but there is still much to be done: the gun barrel fronts and camel backs need to go and always breeders should strive to produce better coats. Dark blues and livers need to be produced and then maybe Swedish and Japanese enthusiasts will stop talking about white Bedlington terriers, for just like a black Bedlington it does not exist. My sincere hope is that show breeders will see the worth of working blood and use it within their breeding programmes, as I can assure them it will improve their results dramatically.

The next thing that needs changing is the attitudes of the KC judges. Already there are some who put up typical dogs, John Holden of Granitor fame being one such judge. Many Bedlington terriers offered for sale in sporting publications and on the internet as working Bedlingtons are in fact show-strain dogs. Seemingly there are a number of people who only care about making some money out of the breed; they care little or nothing at all about the future of the breed and simply breed to sell to an unsuspecting public. Many years ago I went with an acquaintance of mine to look at a potential sire for a heavy type of running dog, certainly not my own favoured type of dog. Anyway, the owner, aware of who I was, turned the conversation round to Bedlington terriers. He had a pair of so-called working-type Bedlington terriers that he showed me. Clearly they were not and then just to reinforce what I already knew he gave me the papers to view. All show bred. I then noticed where the dogs had come from. A show person who at the time I knew very well had let the pair go to a pet home with the express stipulation that the dogs were not be given

A Bedlington brings a wild pig to bay.

away or sold on without prior permission. Not only was that arrangement violated but the new owner sensing a chance of a quick buck bred the pair together and the pups were sold on to an unsuspecting public as working-type Bedlingtons. Not good! Show-bred Bedlingtons will work, but what they will never be is real old-fashioned working-type Bedlington terriers, seeing work from fox to wild boar, by anyone's standards aggressive and testing their quarry.

Around the globe show dogs are seeing some work but we must not stand still and be complacent – to return to the glory days when Bedlington terriers were all truly work or show will take a lot of hard work.

5 Working-Strain Dogs

To my mind the real working strains are Gutchcommon and Rillington respectively. Both of these families of Bedlingtons are working strain as opposed to show blooded. There are also Bedlington terriers that carry some working and show breeding that are essentially of working type. When we speak of working strain some factions in the show world go to great lengths to convince us that no such thing exists and that the show and working-bred dogs are one and the same, and descended from exactly the same root stock. This is ludicrous: the types differ greatly and the Gutchcommon strain of Bedlington terrier is a classic example of how much the two types differ.

All Bedlingtons carry show breeding, but here's the difference: the Gutchcommons are descended from 'old-style' show breeding, typical Bedlington old-type dogs, working-type dogs. All Bedlingtons may have direct links back to Phoebe and Piper those first two Bedlington terriers, but a different type emerged which we now know as the modern show dog. What caused this? I think the blame lies fairly and squarely on the shoulders of the judges. KC judges were picking a newer, altogether more delicate dog, an animal that lent itself to the barber's comb, with a roached back rather than a rise across the loins, tight cat feet and washed-out poor soft coats. Despite the fact Margaret Williamson of Gutchcommon fame was an eminent show judge this good lady was not an admirer of this newer type of dog and despised its totally unterrier-like character and poodle-like appearance. As far as Bedlingtons were concerned, Margaret Williamson had been weaned on a diet of blood and guts working terriers, for her early stock had come from the Misses Maunsell and Hamilton, and they were terriers that would have been tested to the full on all subterranean quarry which invariably meant badger as well as fox.

Margaret Williamson with her
Gutchcommon dogs in Wales.

The earliest Bedlingtons or Rothbury terriers were the gamest of the game and highly prized throughout history as good base lines to produce hard-bitten, albeit totally mute dogs, dogs so hard that they would sooner die rather than give an inch to a badger. Typically this resulted in many dead and disfigured dogs, terriers displaying the classic brock wounds of grey and black healed throat scars or oddly angled jaws that had not quite 'gone back' true. This do-or-die attitude was deemed an asset amongst the fell fox hunters who required only that the red one would die, for theirs was a form of pest control rather than the social event so beloved of the gentry of the southern fox-hunting fraternity. Fell packs hunted in a hostile land with equally hostile terriers; no horsemen followed here, only farmers or gamekeepers on foot whose attitude was that the only good fox was a dead one. That view was widely accepted in Wales too, for the Celtic west traditionally is a hotbed for working Bedlington terriers. Indeed Wales had a reputation, back in the day, for producing extremely hard badger dogs, not only woolly coated Russell types that allegedly contained Bedlington genetic potential but myriad bull-blooded types that would have engaged in such unpleasant pastimes as badger baiting (not to be confused with badger digging) and dog fighting.

Bedlington terriers too had acquitted themselves in the dog pit (as did most hard and aggressive breeds of working terrier), and this in turn led to certain enthusiasts of game and hard terriers crossing Bedlingtons with other terrier breeds. One such breed was the Staffordshire bull terrier, which may or may not have fuelled the rumour of the Bedlington owing some of its ancestry to the old-type pit-fighting bulldog. Certainly the Welsh hybrid Bedlington/Stafford cross bred for this purpose would be highly illegal now. It was said dogs thus bred would bite through the spines of a hedgehog, reducing their mouths to red-blooded slavering jaws and yet crushing the small bodies like a Jack Russell does a rat – truly a high pain threshold!

There is evidence to suggest that this total recklessness and being totally impervious to pain were qualities certain breeders of genuine fox-hunting terriers wanted to encourage in their stock, albeit tempered a little by sounder baying terriers, dogs still with pluck aplenty but with a more sensible, possibly phlegmatic disposition.

Margaret Williamson was undoubtedly inspired by Violet Maunsell and Dorothy Hamilton, people who like Mrs Williamson herself were show judges held in high esteem but with a healthy interest in working Bedlingtons. The Misses Maunsell and Hamilton advertised one of their stud dogs, Heart of Hell, as a show dog that held a working certificate. In fact, in the early part of the twentieth century there were many dogs that could justifiably claim to be both 'work and show'.

Ken Bounden in his book *The Bedlington Terrier* shows a photograph of Champion Sperkeford Jackanapes, and it is that Bedlington in my opinion that epitomises all we should look for in a working-type Bedlington, yet Jackie was a show champion, and an extremely important dog, the founder of the family that one day folk would call Gutchcommon. Jackie was the sire of Margaret Williamson's Musha who in turn was the dam of the famous Worton Demon, the forerunner of the Gutchcommon strain. Worton Demon's sire was Goxhill Blue Boy, a terrier you can directly and accurately trace back to the very first Bedlingtons.

Coats were the primary quality to be valued in all Gutchcommon Bedlingtons; it was something

Pixie, Margaret Williamson's liver bitch.

Margaret Williamson worked hard on right into her winter years, so much so that she believed there was nothing to compare with her beloved strain, though introductions into the line, albeit rare, did occur. Argonauts Blue Pierette, Blythe Blue Red Rover and Dick of Gutchcommon are dogs that are uppermost in my mind. However, in my opinion towards the end some of Mrs Williamson's dogs became less robust and more susceptible to eye problems, and this did nothing to endear the strain to those who favoured the Rillington line of Bedlington, a totally different type of terrier completely in both size and coat. Generally, Rillingtons were much bigger and with substance, though their coats were poorer than the average Gutchcommon in my opinion, but their jaw power and formidable dentistry were magnificent.

Roy Mee the Leicester-based Bedlington breeder adored the Gutchcommon strain with possibly as much affection as Margaret Williamson. I can vividly remember both Rogue of Birkacre and Kentenes Rogue, terriers that were both Gutchcommon and exceptionally coated. John Piggin's Jasper of Kentene was also of this ilk. Up until his death in November 1987 Roy bred and kept some exceptional stock, although I never really had any indication that he actually worked his terriers. John Piggin worked Gutchcommon stock and so did I. In fact it was Piggin who bred The Mad Ratter, a dog I bought from him as a six-week-old liver pup. Born into a world that at the time allowed folk to work fox underground with terriers, Bracken was always destined to work with me. Blessed with a fantastic coat, Bracken was no weed either, for he stood at seventeen inches at the shoulder but was narrow enough to enter

The author's celebrated liver dog The Mad Ratter.

most fox earths. It was pre ban and foxes were numerous, the winters were harsh and my local fox earths were very often occupied. Bracken upon entering his earth had two things on his mind: firstly finding and then attempting to kill his fox, simple as that. He was a model fox-hunting Bedlington, allowing no fox to get past him, either killing or bolting his quarry. I think Margaret Williamson would have liked him.

Dan Russell writing in *Shooting Times & Country Magazine* in March 1979 makes mention of Margaret Williamson's efforts to revive the Bedlington terrier as a working terrier, for the 1970s saw massive interest in the so-called revival of the working Bedlington. It was during this period that the Working Bedlington Terrier Club was formed and George Newcombe was elected the club's Chairman.

As ever the Welsh interest in the breed was massive, and in fact three of the club's prominent committee members were based in Wales: its President, Huw Evans, Secretary and Treasurer, Nigel Beard and Registration and Assistant Secretary, Dave Roberts were all living in Wales at the time.

One of the first areas of controversy and ultimately disagreement amongst Working Bedlington Terrier Club members was the suggestion that the showing of Bedlington terriers at working shows could or would be good publicity for the breed. Ultimately nothing could have been further from the truth and that situation still exists to this day. KC registered dogs were (and still are!) entered into working terrier classes despite there having been no effort to work them, and what is worse judges are often ill prepared or even not qualified to judge the type.

Upon the formation of The Working Type Bedlington Terrier Association, an organisation of which I was Chairman, one of the main objectives was to establish a Judges' Register, a collection of approved, tried and tested working Bedlington judges who absolutely knew what constituted a real old-fashioned working Bedlington. But what indeed is that correct type? Worton Demon from 1923 epitomised it: a long-backed specimen with strong jaws and teeth, and terriers bred from Demon were of his ilk. Mrs Bruce Lowe bred three champions from one litter out of him, Bedlington terriers that were truly work and show dogs.

For those show folk who remember the early Worton and Gutchcommon dogs as show bred it should be mentioned that these self-same show dogs were all descended from working dogs, so it's a little bit like the chicken and the egg concept but with slightly clearer undertones, namely it was always working dogs first and show dogs second in the development of the modern Bedlington terrier. Show

Margaret Williamson's Jemima.

dogs from the early part of the twentieth century were somewhat more typical than today's counterpart.

Newcombe of Rillington, North Yorkshire had undertaken the role of the Working Bedlington Terrier Club's Chairman. George, whom I knew well, would not have taken this appointment on without first considering where the working Bedlington was going in terms of both good publicity and its subsequent improvement. George's arguably most controversial of articles appeared in *The Working Bedlington Terrier Club Journal* number 4 in September 1980 in which he wrote: 'I gather there are two schools of thought on the subject [meaning the improvement of the working-type Bedlington] namely those who think improvement can be made within the breed itself, and those who think that an outcross to another breed will be necessary to revitalise and reintroduce those qualities which the Bedlington has lost. Obviously it would be quicker, and more satisfactory if improvement could be made within the breed, and I think it could to a certain extent, but would it produce what some of us visualise as the perfect Bedlington, re a dog of the correct size and type with good substance, a harsh non trimming coat and sound temperament and real working ability?'

Newcombe was certainly by now beginning to see in his own mind exactly where the working Bedlington was going and he didn't like it.

Not only had Newcombe watched the Bedlington deteriorate to the level of show dog but he had witnessed a shift to rabbiting with the breed rather than the true role of a terrier, namely that of an earth dog, the tod hunter, the taker of foxes.

Indeed Newcombe had become very critical of the really small dogs, the fifteen-inch-and-under-to-the-shoulder terriers who were often too frail to operate in true Bedlington fashion, and criticised them for their lack of bone and subsequently the almost inevitable resulting fault of small teeth set in just as small jaws. George went on to write: 'for this reason I am reluctant to breed with very small dogs.'

George also wrote: 'Thirty years ago there were far more different strains of Bedlingtons available than is the case today (September 1980) and whilst they were not all perfect, several of these strains did produce dogs of the right temperament who certainly had the ability to work.' I wonder why none of these unnamed strains were kept alive

George Newcombe with his dogs.

and worked? It seems nothing short of a tragedy for the breed. Newcombe attributed the demise of the show-type Bedlington to the rumoured poodle breeding.

The late Roy Mee of Leicester maintained that by bastardising the Bedlington with outside blood the progeny could never be called true Bedlingtons, and by the same token Newcombe was calling the show Bedlington the 'pseudo

Pure and outcrossed dogs bred by the author.

Bedlington', and that too could never be called a true Bedlington.

A situation developed that still exists where any hybrid is a working-type Bedlington, but clearly that's not the case for there are some horrendous results of cross-breeding as there are good results of hybridisation. Take for example the almost solid black types, but black has never been a recognised colour for the Bedlington. Black/blue is, but it's a different thing altogether as a true black/blue will have an almost white, silky top knot and not the coat colour of the average Kerry blue terrier. It should be pointed out that these hybridised Bedlingtons should never be called Bedlingtons, just as Roy Mee said all those years ago; neither should it be a Rothbury, or pitmans terrier for that has been done and basically it is the same thing as a Bedlington terrier anyway.

It is not always a good idea for a breed to be named after a place or the creator of the breed, for it can be geographically incorrect and at other times may indicate that just one person is responsible for a type, and whilst that may be true in some cases at other times it can be more appropriate if it is named after a characteristic, for example a wheaten terrier, or a lurcher, a hunting dog who 'lurches' or shows cunning running on quarry. It is for this reason alone I find much favour in calling a new type of Bedlington, a linty coated terrier. It has been a project I have been engaged in for many years now, and it would certainly give us a terrier with which we could work and breed without the constraints of the Kennel Club.

The outcrossed dog will always need pure-bred Bedlingtons, and it makes great sense if these terriers are of the old type as a good number of the hybridised dogs are crossed to modern show-bred dogs, albeit show dogs that work. However I feel that the amount of work that has been done by working terrier enthusiasts who have engaged in cross-breeding should be rewarded by naming a new or re-vamped type of terrier with a alternative name, as regrettably the name Bedlington terrier does in many cases conjure up visions of the show type of dog.

Both Margaret Williamson and George Newcombe voiced the opinion that the show-type Bedlington allegedly contained poodle breeding. Indeed there are also rumours of other breeds being introduced into the Bedlington terrier at various times and I don't mean those that were introduced by outcrossing supporters, as no matter what anyone thinks at least these crosses were well known and quite openly bred.

There is the little matter of brindled Bedlingtons appearing in litters. Some attribute these dogs appearing possibly because of a throw back to early breeding to an old-type fighting bulldog, or bull terrier. Whether one accepts the introduction of bull breeding within the Bedlingtons' early creation has been open to debate for years. Personally I have never supported that notion; however where does the brindle colour come from? Or is it a more modern introduction? If so, again, where does it come from?

Some enthusiasts of the Bedlington terrier support the bull-blood ancestry theory in the breed's early creation based purely upon Staffordshire nailers being in the Rothbury area in the 1800s, and though Black Country workers may have been in the area and brought with them fighting dogs there is no concrete evidence to support the theory. Look at the dogs. I have experience of bull-blooded stock (Staffords) and know several other folk who keep bull stock. There is absolutely no resemblance between the game, broad-mouthed breeds of the English Home Counties and Midlands and the old dogs of Rothbury, the prototype Bedlingtons. Broad chests, round ribs, cat feet, a different genetic type of blue coat, oh no, there's more connection to the whippet than the Bedlington terrier.

Miniature bull terriers, the smaller scaled-down version of the English bull terrier, would be easily absorbed by a Bedlington terrier, with the exception of the full pricked ears, often predominately white colouring and heavy appearance. Here we had a dog with a decent length of leg, long narrow strong head and jaws and a dog that would, as I said before, blend in quite easily with a Bedlington, especially a three-quarter-bred animal. Bull blood from Stafford types may also have been introduced, but I fear this hybrid may have come about for more sinister reasons, namely to produce a fighting or baiting type of dog. Sadly Bedlingtons were fought together too.

Wales seems to be the area where most of the badger-baiting terriers were used. At the end of a badger dig large, powerful dogs were often used to draw the animal from the sett. This terrier was often a Bedlington, a bull breed or sometimes a bull × Bedlington hybrid. Dog fighters would have been drawn to the hardness of such dogs, terriers that were so silent even whilst enduring the most awful punishments imaginable and locked on their adversaries like a bulldog.

Plummer writing in *Rogues and Running Dogs* makes mention of the Staffordshire nailers who moved into the Rothbury area around 1800, although other reports have the date down as a little later. Either way it was said that these hybrids were so bad with other dogs that their owners only exercised them under the cover of darkness. Opinions are divided on the use of bull blood in the Bedlingtons' early make up; the question is, is other bull blood responsible for the supposed brindled Bedlington and just how recent is it? One thing is for certain, if brindled Bedlingtons do exist it's being kept very quiet.

The very early working-strain dogs would certainly have had a greater amount of variation, not just in coat colour but also in shape. Perfect examples are seen in pictures of Ainsley's Piper and of William Clark with his early terriers which show dogs that are not what most of us would immediately recognise as Bedlingtons, in fact Ainsley's dogs look decidedly Border in appearance. Curran Cooper in her clearly self-published pamphlet from 1998 *Warts and All, A Pictorial*

Blyth Bob, a typical old-type Bedlington terrier.

History of the Bedlington Terrier, makes mention of Aynsley (rather than Ainsley) with those previously mentioned dogs, and Curran Cooper states in her opinion these were not Ainsley's (Aynsley's). But, so what? It does show a different type of terrier from those mainly encountered today!

The funny thing is the early Borders looked more fell type and only developed their characteristic otter-type head later, while the early Bedlingtons had a distinct look of later Border about them, that breed then developing the typical Bedlington head we all became so accustomed to. Borders, Bedlingtons and the Dandie Dinmont all come from a common stock and all early specimens were working-strain terriers used on quarry that would fight back, namely otter, fox and badger. John Williams of South Wales has some nice examples of Border/Bedlington hybrids; his dog Basil is just one of them.

The working-strain dogs have for many years been shunned by the show fraternity with these enthusiasts pointing out that the working-strain dogs fail for being not typical with poor leg furnishings and goat coated, and working dog owners merely stating that their dogs are the real thing. There is no doubt whatsoever that good examples of working-strain dogs are *more* typical than their modern-day show counterpart and the working-strain dogs are the real Bedlington terriers. The suggestion that working-strain dogs are in fact show dogs does bear some credence: the fact is once ALL Bedlingtons were work and show, but it was the show fraternity, or more specifically the show judges, that moved the goal posts; fashion saw to the rest and from then the rot set in.

Clearly the late Curran Cooper, a show fancier who in my opinion knew nothing about working dogs but seemingly everything about Bedlingtons, recognised that John Cornforth's Nelson was a show dog, and to quote from her *Warts and All, A Pictorial History of the Bedlington Terrier* he was 'indeed, one who had won his way into *The Kennel Club Stud Book*', yet she goes on to recall that according to the judge, one J.H. Salter, Nelson had weak feet. This is one judge's opinion and maybe it is just one weakness. So what? Alan Minter was a great British middleweight boxer but cut badly around the eyes, but that didn't stop him becoming Middleweight Champion of the World or from being a good boxer. In the same way, Nelson's alleged, and alleged they are, 'weak feet' did not make him a bad example of a Bedlington.

Curran Cooper also got it wrong when she suggested that I as an individual regarded Nelson highly. No, that wasn't me but Dave Parsons who sent me a letter speaking highly of Nelson. In fact the first print I saw of Nelson was when I read Curran Cooper's literary offering! What we should bear in mind is that Bedlington terriers around the year 1882 were real terriers that could justifiably still be described as truly 'work and show'.

What was meant by Salter's comment, weak feet? Weak in what part of the foot? I don't think Curran Cooper understood working dogs. Yes, I can understand if we were talking about the appalling examples of some weedy show specimens, then weak feet would be a problem as they would not have been able to 'leg it' quickly enough away from some quarry with a sharp end, or simply because they hadn't the necessary fire and guts to engage a pre-ban fox. What is the one quality, if you were allowed only just one single prime requisite, you would desire in a working terrier? I don't think, I know, most folk would say good dentistry; it is the single most necessary quality any working terrier needs. For the working Bedlington terrier to succeed in its cause it needs to be handled by real terrier men and women, folk who will work them, and if it is exempted hunting then it's exempted hunting until the day the law changes, if it ever does, but work these dogs we must always do.

It will never keep its status as a working dog if it lies in the hands of uncaring folk who actually want and ask for a white Bedlington. How ludicrous and how wrong! The play actors always get found out, and the lies will always come out. Real hunters talk the truth, their very dialect eats and breathes the fields, the fells, the mountains. From fen land to forest, coast to the inner cities hunters talk the same thing – working terriers. Their passion knows no bounds, their dogs are their lives. God bless the working Bedlington terrier. This breed, this very valiant breed did not forge its awesome reputation by chasing rabbits alone, though the pretenders, the five-minute wonders would have you believe so. As I said, God bless the working Bedlington terrier.

6 Outcrossing

It was George Newcombe of Rillington, North Yorkshire who first thought up the idea of hybridising or outcrossing Bedlington terriers. George always maintained it was nothing at all to do with improving coats, teeth or jaw power and certainly not working instinct. Newcombe had hit a point in time when he needed fresh blood in his line and he had a choice: modern show stock or Gutchcommon-bred Bedlingtons. George had used the latter in the past and decided not to do so again; to be fair he didn't like the strain that much, deploring its sulky temperament (a little unkindly as it goes, I feel), its pointed bottom jaw (a problem manifested in later years with the strain) and its slowness to start work. The show dogs offered somewhat less, and like Margaret Williamson he disliked the short camel backs, barrel ribs, cat feet and abysmal coats.

The show folk were already claiming there was no difference between the working strain and the show dogs, and that they all came from the same source, namely Piper and Phoebe. What they didn't acknowledge is fashion (brought about by KC judges) had dictated to the show people what would win, and when a typical dog didn't win the goal posts were moved. Breeders had a choice to win and breed this new untypical (faulty) Bedlington or not win, deviate away from the show bench, be alienated and somewhat isolated. One breeder is understood to have said if the judges didn't pick this particular kennel's dogs then that kennel would breed the elegant newer poodle-type of dog.

Clearly none of this impressed George, so when the time came for new blood, Newcombe, as controversial as ever, dropped his bombshell and quit the Working Bedlington Terrier Club where he had held the post of Chairman. The working Bedlington world reeled when George suggested bringing in outside terrier blood and thus began the process we now refer to collectively as outcrossing. Newcombe's first attempts were with pedigree Lakeland breeding, for George already had a

Bedlington × Lakeland hybrid. Roger Fowler's well-known working terrier, the late Ted, killed whilst working underground.

thriving kennel of both Bedlington terriers and Lakelands. George was overjoyed with his first-cross animals, one a blue dog going on to become Norman, probably the most famous Bedlington hybrid ever.

He didn't stop there, going on to breed Tarka, a liver-coloured dog and latterly Ringo, Dart and Venus. (In fact John Piggin bred the latter but Newcombe had the bitch in lieu of a stud fee.) In later years George tried a different cross, one by dint of Border terrier blood. George Newcombe had made friends with several people who were like minded and had experimented with several differing hybrids. One Dave Parsons had experimented around with Border/Lakeland, whippet and dachshund breeding, while others stuck with the original cross of Lakeland or unregistered fell terrier breeding. I experimented with the Irish breed the Glen of Imaal terrier and also pedigree Lakeland terrier.

Another hunter from Chester had used black fell terrier, something George would not have endorsed. Eventually almost a bandwagon had trundled into the working Bedlington world for very shortly myriad horrendous crosses had started to mount up: Kerry blue, Staffordshire bull terriers, Jack Russells were being suggested and even horror of horrors wire-haired fox terriers.

Had the outcrossing world gone mad? We were rapidly approaching the day of the Bedlington mongrel! We certainly already had dogs, black fell terrier like with undocked tails, masquerading as working-type Bedlingtons, something they could never be. I myself used two lines of experimental hybrids, the one in collaboration with George Newcombe that was a line to Irish-bred Glen of Imaal terriers. George voiced the opinion that the long flexible back of the Glen would be a good addition to improving Bedlington types. So it was that I was encouraged by George to use a working Glen of Imaal terrier as an outcross. To be honest I wasn't really trying to breed a Bedlington, rather a dog reminiscent of a prototype Rothbury terrier, an animal that spawned both the Bedlington, Dandie Dinmont terrier and to a degree the Border terrier.

My outcrosses did produce variance in coat colour including grizzles and black-nosed reds (something prototype Bedlington types also did). I bred using only Sam, a blue/black dog with a terrific punishing head on him and a coat texture to behold, and it was this dog that I used to

Sam, a first-cross Bedlington/Glen of Imaal.

Bedlington × Jack Russell owned by Leon Robinson.

Newcombe's Donna. The resulting pups were superb examples of heavyweight Bedlingtons. What's more they worked and worked well too.

Newcombe had continued work with his Lakeland and fell terrier breeding programmes, and then decided to use Borders, going on to say it was probably easier to find a typical Border terrier than it was a 'proper' Lakeland terrier.

This is an appropriate time to mention the other crosses with the Bedlington that are rather more one-offs or novelty hybrids. The Bedlington × Jack Russell has been used several times. The legendary Bert Gripton had involvement with this cross as does Leon Robinson, the sporting Lucas terrier aficionado from Milton Keynes. Indeed Leon has a dog of this breeding which is a dynamite worker.

Staffordshire bull terrier × Bedlington terrier is by no means unknown either. However I feel this hybrid has nothing to offer the outcrossing projects being practised by various parties. It would make for an interesting hard-bitten working terrier, and I believe this hybrid was a type used in the South Wales coalfields. In contrast to this last statement one could, I suppose, counter this by stating that both the Bedlington and Stafford are game enough in any case and that neither needed additions of pure guts and fire from either breed.

I recently saw an advertisement for Bedlington × Kerry blue pups. Back in the day Kerrys did some work that usually meant something very unpleasant and equally illegal, but nowadays ALL badger work is against the law. Nevertheless it does prove that the breed have pure fire and gameness. Like all the Irish terrier breeds it may have been used in illegal dog fighting. All this indicates the terrier is an immensely hard breed. Nonetheless few Kerrys are worked in modern times although one does see the rare advertisement for Kerry blue × greyhound lurchers. Those Bedlington × Kerry blue pups might make for an interesting starting point for a lurcher breeding project, although you have the ideal lurcher base line in a Bedlington in any case, don't you!

The Dandie Dinmont terrier is another breed that has been used in hybridisation with the Bedlington; it is after all the nearest related breed to the Bedlington although extremely few Dandies appear to be worked nowadays. It does however still have potential for producing a type of terrier reminiscent of the old Rothbury Forest dog. The indications are that the Dandie Dinmont terrier played some part in the creation of the miniature wire-haired dachshund and therefore could be a related breed to a greater or lesser degree to the Bedlington terrier. Recently I saw an advert for a variance of a reverse three-quarter-bred terrier/running dog where the sire was a Dandie Dinmont and the dam was a Bedlington × whippet.

Arguably the whippet could be a related breed to the Bedlington terrier, as certainly the two breeds are inextricably intertwined though whether the latter of the two played any part in the whippet's creation is open to debate. It may be so, but I don't believe the whippet contributed anything to the Bedlington. It is true though that early whippet types also included not only traditional smooth but also rough small lurcher types. As the reader can see, over the years a fair few breeds have been crossed with the Bedlington terrier, some having the potential to produce a improved type of working dog, whilst others are, it seems, totally inappropriate.

Since writing my first book *The Working Bedlington* I have been accused of doing a U-turn on the practice of outcrossing, so it is now time to clear this up once and for all. First of all I think there is a place for hybridising and a very valid case for it too. Secondly I think it is of vital importance for us to preserve the pure-bred Bedlington terrier at all costs, as just in lurcher or longdog breeding we need pure-bred grey-hounds and whippets, so in outcrossing we need pure Bedlingtons. It is a vital key ingredient and is imperative on the road to improving the show-type dog. The show world will not, quite obviously, entertain cross-bred dogs but a correct type of pure-bred dog may be acceptable. So what? OK, why indeed, but I still feel it would be nice to see dogs that win in the show ring that would work well and be of the correct original working type.

Wouldn't that be great! The show folk would have a sounder dog and it would take away the frustration from us who call ourselves working terrier folk who cringe when we see people trying to sell pups as work or show dogs. OK, show dogs can work, and you will get one to work, but what you cannot do is rectify physical faults. I have covered this subject fully in my chapter on working-strain dogs.

We have now arrived at a time when we have several different types of outcrossing practices and the danger is that we produce a mongrel rather than a Bedlington or Rothbury-type terrier. So where's the solution? There is one. Is the practice of outcrossing worth following? Yes it is. Why? Because an improved type of terrier can be achieved. I have already stated that the pure correct type of working Bedlington needs saving at all costs; it is as vital to the improved terrier as the greyhound or whippet is to the bastard greyhound, which is of course called the lurcher. The bastard Bedlington could assume another name. The Bedlington and Rothbury have already been used so we can't have either of those, but what we can have is the linty coated terrier. It is the perfect name for the specifically bred working terrier with an extremely strong Bedlington influence. Brian Plummer did a similar thing with Jack Russell types that he developed along different lines that went on to be named after him, namely the

Plummer terrier. The same thing happened in the creation of the sporting Lucas terrier as opposed to the Lucas terrier.

Therefore I suggest the linty coated terrier as the name given to improved types. A working standard certainly needs setting up and adhering to but we should not call it a Bedlington, and why would we want to when the linty coated terrier is the perfect name? Once the standard is set up and dedicated parties are striving to breed it the results could be remarkable. Outcrossing is I feel a worthy project, but it's just that we should not call them Bedlingtons in my opinion, and it may be the greatest tribute to all the folk who breed them if we set up a standard, adhere to it and clear out the mongrel element. Hybrid dogs work incredibly well, have potential to provide a sound and wide working gene pool, and it would be the greatest accolade to the enthusiasts who breed such dogs to rewrite the name completely and christen the dogs linty coated terriers.

When Brian Plummer spoke of his Plummer terriers and said they are not Jack Russells I saw a similar situation with outcrossed Bedlington hybrids. We see terriers that are clearly not Bedlingtons and the biggest example of this is the so-called black Bedlington. No such thing exists, for it is out of keeping with an old-type Bedlington as is the white Bedlington, something we see time and time again in show-bred dogs. The black hybrid terrier is one I confess I do actually like, as it is a very attractive terrier and it works well. Black-nosed reds occasionally occur as do blue and red grizzle, but none is a recognised Bedlington colour, just as black and tan isn't, but all these do crop up in outcrossed terriers. Could there have been this colouration in prototype Bedlington terriers? Surely there is no reason why such dogs cannot be incorporated in the 'new' breed that may or may not be termed a linty coated terrier. I think the project is an exciting and very viable ongoing venture and it is one I will watch with great interest.

Plummer succeeded in breeding a new type of dog of a Jack Russell type in appearance, and there is no greater incentive for outcrossed Bedlington devotees to do a similar thing with their wards that could just prove to be the ultimate working terrier with a very heavy Bedlington influence. It is a fact of life that a great number of serious working Bedlington men and women now favour outcrossed dogs, and the aforementioned black as opposed to black/blue dog is one I confess

Brothers in arms, a Bedlington and Border terrier go about their work in Slovakia. Related breeds that could have easily been called Coquetdale terriers.

I like very much. I recently went ferreting with an enthusiast from Wales with a brace of such dogs. To me they were not Bedlington terriers per se but that is not taking anything away or detracting from these terriers' attraction or viability; in fact nothing could be further from the truth. A number of people now see the modern Bedlington as a travesty and there is no denying it is a mere shadow of the show dog of the early twentieth century. I know that a certain element abhor the comparison between their dogs and the modern show Bedlington. I myself have voiced this opinion, and it is for this reason that I suggest that if a uniform type can be created then a fantastic possibility opens itself up.

The cross with the Border terrier offers many great options, for not only is the Border a related breed to both the Bedlington and Dandie Dinmont terrier but it does bear a resemblance to the very early prototype Bedlingtons. John Williams of Swansea has dogs of great potential and, more importantly, they are of a type that works; they contain some Lakeland breeding, certainly in one case that I know of (from Newcombe's Venus) and an addition from John Holden's Granitor-bred dogs. Few have seized on the possibility that Border blood has much to offer as John Williams has done, but I really do rate Williams' dogs for type and viability; you could say he has carried on with a project left by the late George Newcombe.

Newcombe, always controversial and always outspoken, did however have a habit of moving the goal posts when it suited him, for example he abhorred the modern show-bred dog yet persuaded John Piggin to breed a second litter from Lady Lena of Eakring, the reason being Newcombe had lost a pup from an initial litter due to a stomach virus, or so he said.

John Piggin agreed and once again used Norman to Lena to breed Venus, a large poor-coated full fading blue and tan, but despite being three-quarter Lakeland I never personally saw any advantage or improvement for the so-called working-type Bedlington, or as it should have more accurately been termed, outcrossed terrier. Venus had Stanolly (modern show blood and Gutchcommon blood), and if anyone else had used this breeding I think Newcombe would have criticised them severely.

The black fell terrier though strictly speaking a coloured northern terrier and extremely easy to enter does carry white-bodied genetic material, namely Jack Russell or bull blood, and because of this is

Lady Lena of Eakring, the late John Piggin's bitch. Newcombe used her in his outcrossing projects.

unsuitable for the improvement of the Bedlington. The cross will produce effective one-off working hybrids but will contribute nothing to the cause of the Bedlington or linty coated terrier if this is what we decide to call the outcrossed terrier.

7 The Bedlington Lurcher

*The night is dark and the wind blows cold, the trees sway to and fro, the
battery is charged the dog is at large and tomorrow we shall have stew.*

My obsession is running dogs. It really always has been: I grew
up around racing greyhounds and my first running dog was a
whippet, a beautiful blue brindle bitch called Gyp. God bless
that dog (or should that be goddess as in the goddess of hunting,
Diana) for Gyp and I enjoyed considerable success, and it also paved
the way to my love of the
Bedlington terrier.

I grew up in an old mining
town with a massive working
dog culture, my own family
keeping lurchers, whippets,
greyhounds, various terriers
and ferrets. It was as working
class as could be, socialist to
the core, yet a more field
sports-inspired community
you could not find. In Britain
in those days before the
Hunting Act, when you
could hunt both the fox and
the hare, it was usual to go
out and hunt, catch, and try
new quarry.

I had discovered lurchers
and had hunted with one
alongside my whippet and a
springer spaniel and my old

*Bedlington-bred lurcher pictured with a
working terrier of the day, between the two
World Wars.*

76

trusty Sealyham-type Russell bitch, Sue. But the years had rolled by and rabbit and pre-ban hare hunters (not to mention fox) were using spot lamps to secure their catches. Enter Blue, a quarter-bred Bedlington and reputedly out of a famous first-cross Bedlington × greyhound, Spring (immortalised in E.G. Walshe's epic book *Lurchers & Longdogs*). A friend Fred Newman had her, bred a litter and offered her to me, so I can hardly take any credit for her hunting prowess, but what it did do is open the door for me to the working Bedlington, and with my growing interest in Bedlington lurchers so grew my fascination with the pure-bred Bedlington.

I had worked Blue on rabbit, rat, fox and hare, shown her winning the Cottesmore Hunt show for twenty-two-inch and under rough bitch class, and bred her to a classy whippet/greyhound. This was the foundation to a line of Bedlington lurcher where I only ever introduced pure sight hound and Bedlingtons or hybrids between the two. I managed to produce eventually a strain of blue and liver rough-coated lurchers that were the most effective predatory dogs I have ever personally known; but that was a different project to that conductd by most Bedlington lurcher breeders. To many enthusiasts a lurcher usually means a straightforward hybrid between a working Bedlington (or show dog) and a whippet (very often), or even better a greyhound.

Obviously I had to hybridise Bedlingtons to pure sight hounds to bring this into my line of lurcher, and I did it on a couple of occasions, once to a whippet (both my dogs) and also to a greyhound. That latter litter was a match made in heaven; I used the famous liver dog The Mad Ratter to a very well-bred Irish greyhound out of the acclaimed dog Linda's Champion. The resulting pups were fantastic hunting lurchers on all quarry, excelling not only on rabbit but also on pre-ban hare and fox. Two went to Gary Taylor of Markfield, a brindle called Tod and a blue/black called Bullet. I eventually used Tod back to my own small rough bitch called Rush who was a granddaughter of dear old Blue. The resulting pup was death on four legs for both rabbits and hares – she was just about ideal, a power runner with great stamina measuring twenty-three inches at the shoulder. Her name was Goldie and she worked fur and feather, with ferrets and loved to pick up for the gun. Goldie was a great dog for me.

Back to Bedlington × greyhounds. Generally speaking the hybrid levels out uniformly in type – litter wastage is not encountered, all genuine ones are always, but always, rough coated (if you are offered a smooth one it's not a first cross), usually black/blue in colour but sometimes red/fawn and on odd occasions brindle. The same applies in Bedlington × whippets, the only difference being the lurcher is much, much smaller!

John Glover's working Bedlington lurchers.

Three-quarter-bred specimens do find much more variance though, and rough coats often give way to broken or smooth coats, and the colours vary too (as can height). White-bodied dogs occur as do other colours, from part-coloured through to blues, blue/blacks, brindles and reds or mask-faced light fawns. Generally speaking the three-quarter greyhound/ Bedlington was regarded as a more viable pre-ban hare dog with some specimens reaching up to twenty-eight inches at the shoulder, this of course being an added bonus for the pre-ban fox hunter.

Bedlington blood brought with it more than enough fire to make an efficient fox dog with both F1 and F2 hybrids excelling at fox hunting. To this day the first-cross Bedlington × greyhound is probably *the* Bedlington lurcher to own, for in these times of rat and rabbit hunting only, this type excels at both of these quarry species both day and night, and it also works well with ferrets.

In my experience the greyhound version of the Bedlington lurcher is the one to breed, buy or own. There is no denying the Bedlington × whippet is a very typical-looking traditional type of rabbiting dog, nonetheless I do have reservations about this dog. It's a kind of wasted hybrid for it's not as good as the terrier at the terriers' game, and certainly not as good as the pure whippet as a running dog. I have bred a litter of first-cross Bedlington/whippets and kept back one for my own use, eventually using him in my strain of Bedlington lurchers.

Whippets are often crossed with Bedlingtons. There is no faster dog than the whippet over the first twenty yards. The author's dog Jude.

Bedlington × whippet. The well-known bitch Rags owned by Laurie Ferguson.

However at twenty-one inches at the shoulder and a very sturdy build, he did resemble a small Bedlington/greyhound hybrid. I also bred a couple of three-quarter whippet, quarter Bedlington litters and the resulting pups turned out all smooth coated and reminiscent of pure-bred whippets.

Bedlington/whippet hybrids can and do work, and really look the part. In fact, it is a very attractive hybrid, and on looks alone I like them, but there is nothing that the Bedlington/whippet can do that the pure-bred whippet can't do better. The only thing I will say is you may get a better skin than that of the smooth-coated whippet. It is my opinion that the pure-bred whippet is the ultimate mini lurcher, that is to say twenty-one inches at the shoulder and lower.

First-cross Bedlington × greyhound, the ideal all-rounder.

A typical Bedlington lurcher.

Genuine Bedlington/whippet hybrids are however much sought after and sell tremendously well, especially bitch pups. As a lurcher it will work and it will catch, and it should double up as a gun dog and assist on beats, but then again so will a whippet and indeed a Bedlington/greyhound.

My bitch Blue was reputedly a daughter of Spring, that aforementioned famous dog. I hope she was for Spring was a lovely looking dog. He epitomised a typical Bedlington/greyhound, blue and rough of coat, had a real traditional look about him, and most lurchers thus bred seem to be of this stamp. Gary Taylor's Bullet certainly was; he had an exceptionally racy look about him and caught enough pre-ban hares. His litter brother Tod had tremendous stamina and worked the spectrum of rabbit, hare and fox.

Most Bedlington/greyhounds level out at around twenty-two to twenty-five inches at the shoulder, breed remarkably true to type and can be relied upon with careful entering, conditioning and care to make efficient vermin exterminators. I like to use a Bedlington male to the running dog bitch (this would equally apply with a whippet version of the cross); in the case of a greyhound version I like small Irish-bred dams and a good-coated working-strain Bedlington. I don't worry if he is a large Bedlington, for large sires appear within working stock, and in fact you can have two litter brother male Bedlingtons where one can be large whilst the other very much along true terrier size. The tendency for this to manifest itself has always happened, and I attribute it to a scent hound ancestor back in the Bedlingtons' ancestry, a dog of the otterhound type (it is no coincidence Bedlingtons are extremely aquatic dogs).

Whether your dam is a sprinter or distance dog matters little I feel for the lurcher is a totally different ball game, possessing hybrid vigour that will give the dog its staying power. You do need speed however – I must be honest I have always rated speed as an essential quality in any working running dog. On that very subject I think I should mention that I wouldn't personally recommend three-quarter reverse breds, that is to say Bedlington × Bedlington/sighthound (whippet or greyhound) as I think speed has been sacrificed. You may as well have an outsized Bedlington and work that (it has been done).

The real deal is the first-cross Bedlington/greyhound. It possesses everything: ideal size, good coat, constitution and pre ban was an efficacious fox dog. I remember a red bitch called Belle who was murderous on fox; she wasn't in any way a mixer but killed with efficiency. However, one night she mistimed her throat hold and took her fox across the loins. It was obvious she had severed an artery and by the time her handler reached her the whole scene was one of carnage, with lots of blood obviously from the fox but also from the bitch as the fox had turned slashing her ear, and the blood from her ears mixed with that of the fox making for a scene reminiscent of a medieval execution.

The bigger genuine three-quarter greyhound/Bedlington also has its devotees and was popular amongst some pre-ban hare hunters. The cross also excelled on fox, not to mention, it is said, illegal activities on deer. A guy once told me about a Bedlington/greyhound × greyhound he had bought. The bitch was five years old and I believe family problems had forced her unfortunate sale. The lurcher had excelled at rabbits on the lamp, bringing back all her catches alive and unharmed, and she had also worked hare (pre ban) both daylight and on the beam,

Ferret kits and all potential workers, the essential aid to a rabbiting dog. All Bedlingtons should be broken to ferrets.

her party trick apparently being that whilst her owner fed his ponies the dog would jump out of the window of his vehicle, catch a hare in the dark and it would be delivered for the hunter when he returned back to his vehicle after evening equine duties!

Rabbits are the staple quarry in modern times, and provided the hunter has permission to catch rabbits off any given property then it's all fairly straightforward and legal. Rabbits can be caught with either dogs or ferrets totally legally, and lurchers and ferrets go together like bacon and eggs. It is the ideal combination in fact. Most hunters know the score but for the absolute beginner a few simple guidelines should suffice. They are as follows. Always start your team with youngsters, that is to say ferret kit and pup, bring up both together, allow both to drink from the same bowl. Don't bring in a big hob ferret and allow it to bite a pup – as I say youngsters in both cases. I shall cover entering and ferreting in my chapter on the quarry.

Both Bedlington lurcher versions (whippet and greyhound) can and should work with ferrets and lamp rabbits and rats. There are variances on the lurcher types I have described which I shall examine now, including hybrid Bedlington sires or dams paired to either whippets or greyhounds, pure Bedlingtons mated to either salukis or deerhounds and Bedlingtons paired to hybrid longdogs, most notably so the whippet/greyhound cross. The whippet/greyhound hybrid is one I freely confess I like in its basic first cross as it is blessed with speed (a quality I rate highly) and is an extremely adept catcher of rabbits. Pre ban these hybrids often put up a surprisingly good show when run with both saluki and saluki/greyhound hybrids. It is one purpose-bred whippet hybrid I really rate and one I would breed, keep and work. But here's the snag: whilst the hybrid mated to a Bedlington would undoubtedly breed rabbiting dogs a genuine first-cross Bedlington/greyhound would be a better proposition. The reason once again is that you give up too much size.

Saluki hybrids with Bedlingtons have been tried in the past. Fred Newman of Hinkley had two red bitches that were saluki × Bedlington/greyhound, and these variations on the three-quarter-bred running dog were very effective pre-ban fox dogs. Saluki × Bedlington hybrids have also been experimented with, and I actually think there may be potential there as long as tractability has not been sacrificed. Deerhound × Bedlingtons (if you can successfully mate them) do, when the cross has been made, produce exceptionally beautiful lurchers that would of course work, but all that said the genuine Bedlington/ greyhound takes some beating. Another variation is the mating of a Bedlington to a longdog such as a saluki/greyhound or deer-hound greyhound, both of which are fifty per cent sight hound and fifty per cent terrier.

Bedlington hybrids have been mated often enough to both grey-hounds and particularly whippets, but for some reason the idea of a lurcher breeding with a Lakeland terrier (or Border or indeed Glen of Imaal) doesn't quite jell! I once thought about allowing my whippet dog to be used for free on a Border/Lakeland type a friend had, but I am glad we decided against it. If I have reservations about the Bedlington/whippet hybrid then God forbid the mating of Border terriers and whippets together, and the same applies with Lakelands too in my opinion.

It does seem however that when starting a lurcher breeding project most lurcher breeders look to three-quarter-bred Bedlington/Lakelands when using a Bedlington hybrid as opposed to a pure Bedlington. Les Robinson did this years ago when he bred a litter from his large three-quarter-bred Bedlington/Lakeland bitch, Amy, to a well-known whippet/greyhound. Although the resulting pups were technically fifty per cent terrier, fifty per cent running dog both parents were crosses, and I think most folk would rather have a genuine first cross. As always I would advise a Bedlington/greyhound.

Another facet of Bedlington lurcher breeding is the mating together of two Bedlington-blooded lurchers, for example Bedlington/greyhound × Bedlington/whippet. Of course this means the would-be buyer is totally at the mercy of the vendor's honesty regarding their puppies' parentage, for various lurchers can look one thing and yet in reality be anything but. At least in a genuine first-cross litter you should be looking at a pure-bred whippet or greyhound nursing the litter, and in a ideal situation you may get to see the Bedlington stud

By its very shape and running style the Bedlington makes a sound lurcher breeding base.

dog. A lot of people do breed two Bedlington lurchers together however, and the most commonly practised one is the mating of a first cross to a second cross, thereby producing a five-eighths running dog, three-eighths terrier – a very popular type of lurcher.

Just occasionally one hears of Italian greyhounds that have been mated to whippets, which is a strange idea for all the Italian greyhounds I have seen have been very frail, skinny and fine boned, and hardly conducive to producing game little running dogs. Other suggestions and rare examples include the Italian greyhound/Bedlington hybrid, very often using the Italian greyhound sire to the Bedlington dam. This cross is not advised even if the running dog side is in actual fact an Italian greyhound/whippet hybrid as is sometimes found.

Suffice to say if I voice concerns about the viability of the Bedlington/whippet hybrid I am hardly going to endorse the use of the Italian greyhound, for the breed is a toy one and this is as ludicrous as suggesting

An alert Bedlington-bred lurcher gazes the field for potential prey.

using English toy terriers for ratting! Whether anyone nowadays works Italian greyhounds is debatable, however we can be sure the nature of this diminutive sight hound is totally different to that of a working whippet, and those that engaged in breeding programmes involving Italian greyhound/whippet hybrids were extremely suspect. I certainly would not advise the use of Italian greyhounds in the production of mini lurchers.

Nowadays with internet access it is relatively easy to find pups for sale and I must say there are a good number of genuine Bedlington lurchers on the market. *Exchange & Mart* used to be the publication to check, and now *The Countryman's Weekly* is a great starting point to look for lurchers for sale.

The alternative to buying is breeding a litter yourself and many people do, but a breeding project is very much of an eye opener if you have never done it before. Make no mistake you may well make some good friends along the way but you will also collect an entourage of eccentrics, fools and general time wasters – it's all par for the course I'm afraid. Nevertheless, it still remains one of the most satisfying things in field sports to breed, nurture and eventually catch with a dog you have bred yourself.

Greyhounds are still relatively easy to obtain, but on the ethics side what do you do with your greyhound dam after you have bred her? Generally speaking the lot of a retired greyhound can be pretty bad, save for those in the care of the dedicated rehoming and rescue centres who do a fantastic job. Personally I think you owe your bitch a great debt once she has been mated, carried her whelps and reared them. What's more, greyhounds do make delightful hunting partners given the chance; however the reader should be aware we are talking about a pure sight hound here and not a lurcher. Owners of whippets would jell with such hounds however. Anyway, the greyhound certainly deserves better than what a lot of them get.

Getting a successful mating between a Bedlington and a greyhound can be quite difficult at times: it took several hours to mate The Mad Ratter who stood sixteen inches at the shoulder to a twenty-eight-inch greyhound. However with wooden platforms and patience it can work, but it is probably one of the reasons why a lot of people pair Bedlingtons and whippets together. If ever there was a reason for allowing a young stud dog to mate a bitch early on in its life then this could be it; there are others of course.

Indeed when do you allow a young dog to serve a bitch? As soon as the sap has risen basically. Most serious hunters or breeders of dogs keep a dog for life, full stop. All my stud dogs served bitches early on in life, and it never hurt them or stopped them working, and it actually promoted the breed or type as the case may have been. There is nothing worse than a stud dog who doesn't know what he is doing and it does happen. Four, five and six-year-old virgin dogs often fail to serve their bitch. Why wait? Nature doesn't. If the breeding is good why would you cap it? A bitch may be different, but a stud dog, no.

Whatever route you choose, the breeding or buying direction, eventually you are going to be in the position where you have an inoculated pup and you are standing in the field and saying 'what now?' For the benefit of those who have never yet been in this situation I will go through the basic principles you should follow between inoculation and entering to rabbit. Let us fast forward to the time the pup has gone through its inoculations. You have socialised your whelp (very important), he/she returns to call immediately, your games of throwing paper balls up to a solid ball, and eventually dummies, are paying off, your animal retrieves as a matter of course. You have got your charge drinking from the same bowl as the ferret and have taught the basic commands of sit and stay, etc. All is looking good. It is never too early to let a pup have a look. Now this comes at a very topical time for me, for at the time of writing I am training up a well-bred whippet pup. OK, it's not a lurcher, but we are talking about diminutive dogs of nineteen inches to twenty-five inches at the shoulder (in the main) so I am going to use this dog as a yardstick. Given that this dog is to be used in all-round rabbit, rat and gun dog work I think this would be an ideal running dog to use as an example.

Early entering. Usually this is not recommended and there is good reasoning why in a running dog. Some dogs, especially larger running dogs such as deerhounds for example, take a long time to mature and their bones and muscles to develop fully; however in a smaller dog such as a small lurcher or whippet this is not so acute. With a rookie dog trainer the temptation can be to early enter, but sometimes this can be the ruination of a dog when an animal is overmatched on superior quarry, and a fit, fully grown winter rabbit can be just that. For dogs to watch rabbits caught in ferreters' purse nets certainly helps them to understand what it is all about. Similarly, to watch rabbits not fully grown, those winged when out shooting and of course rabbits suffering with myxomatosis. All these examples build confidence in a young dog; it turns them into workaholic running dogs and sharpens their keenness no end.

My own whippet pup, a dog bred in the purple by Jeff Hutchings of Pennymeadow Whippets, actually caught his first rabbit at ten weeks of age, a tiny hamster-sized babe barely out of its nest who bumbled

The staple quarry of most and still unaffected by the current hunting laws – the humble rabbit.

into the path of the equally innocent and green whippet pup. The pup Jude caught the unfortunate mini rabbit and brought it back to me – what success. What do you do? It's an accident and it should not have happened, but it has. Part of my job is pest control so there isn't a month of the year I don't get rabbits. Usually I shoot these with my .22 rimfire rifle, so as a consequence Jude accompanied me on lots of rabbit forays, his confidence grew and he started to pick up for me retrieving both dead and winged conies plus shot pheasants and partridges. Myxomatosis came to one area and Jude quickly nailed two affected rabbits, one on the lamp when I went out on a reconnaisance trip prior to ferreting (incidentally this is a great way to find out rabbit numbers on any given tract of land). On this particular night whilst checking out numbers I took the pup along more for a bit of exercise. Well, we spotted and easily caught a myxied rabbit, and a few days earlier he nailed another in the daytime – both very easy.

I had started him ferreting, but to be honest I have never been a fan of ferreting first especially when your running dog is to be used at night primarily (irrespective of breed or type) as the tendency can be as a lamping dog it will carry on hunting up when it misses a rabbit on the beam. At around seven months I let him have a go at a couple of squatters on the beam, easy rabbits though he missed them, but he was very close and certainly not outmatched. At just over eight months he got lucky and caught his first rabbit, which he duly retrieved to hand. To say I was over the moon would be a massive understatement. Not long after this I mentioned this event on an internet forum site, and you can probably imagine how some (but not all) reacted to a sapling of such a tender age catching. Yet it was OK, he is not a dog who opens up and he clearly was not overmatched.

That does not happen all the time. Your Bedlington/greyhound may well be ready at eight months or it may be eighteen months; the key is to let your dog let you know, which you will get a feeling for when you are out in the field. Running dogs often enter early and it is true that some get ruined. Terriers are a totally different thing, and there are occasions when some Bedlingtons don't want to know until they are three years of age or more. Pushing and overmatching will surely ruin a dog, so in the case of a beginner it is probably best to wait that bit longer. Although premature entering can ruin a running dog I have never heard of one hurt by late entering, and here again another story should suffice.

I had a lovely rough-coated liver-coloured Bedlington lurcher called Leo. The dog had matured nicely and was about a year old when my marriage broke up and subsequently a divorce ensued, and although I took the dogs out on exercise I certainly had a lot going on in my life. Anyway, after things all got sorted I once again turned my attention to working the dog. My son had worked him in the daytime whilst I was at work but now Leo was around two years of age, a windy night beckoned and Leo wed to rabbits, instantly catching them and it was so easy he never looked back. By two-and-a-half to three years he was out of this world, an excellent pot provider and vermin dog. As I said I have never heard of a dog ruined by late entering.

I shall talk more about methods used to secure conies with dogs including ferreting and lamping in the next chapter on the quarry. As a pot provider the Bedlington lurcher takes some beating; as a beautiful, traditional-looking lurcher it is bettered by none.

8 The Quarry

I have always been a hunter. It is a very primeval thing, a very natural feeling – man the hunter gatherer; and the pursuit of game, vermin, fish, feathered and fur has fascinated me for as long as I can remember. I can remember the first thing I ever killed (a mouse), my first fish (a bream) and so on. As I say, a natural thing. Then we find dogs, God bless them. My great grandad used to quote a well-used saying, doubtless repeated to many over the years: 'Dogs got a cleaner mouth than you, never told a lie.' As I said, we find dogs, and for me it would always be working dogs.

I have never owned any other type of dog than either running dogs or terriers for I have never needed to. Both of these will do every task you need from them in the hunting or working field and that includes doubling as gun dogs. Despite the fact that this is a book about terriers I have decided to include references to running dog quarry too, and this will include the brown hare (though Bedlingtons have been used successfully on this species too) and its taking by lurchers which is now forbidden in the UK, so I have included it in a historical context as it was all pre ban. Fox work with Bedlington lurchers will also be looked at, again in a historical context and therefore also pre ban.

It should also be mentioned that Bedlington lurchers have been used in the past on various species of deer. I should also hasten to add this practice is once again illegal and is mentioned purely to give a full picture of what has happened in the past. Let me reiterate the taking of deer with any running dog or lurcher is illegal and therefore should NEVER be attempted. But in fact muntjac, roe and fallow have all been targeted by hunters with lurchers in the past and pre ban.

The Bedlington terrier is often described as a jack of all trades, but I don't like that description for it implies the dog is not quite as capable of being good at a specific job, which is a nonsense. With the current laws in the UK regarding hunting and the working of dogs we are in a position where the only unrestricted hunting is to the rat and rabbit. Badger work is totally forbidden in the UK, and the only thing you can do now is look at a badger sett; other than that it's all illegal. Fox work is classed as exempted hunting and therefore reliant on various criteria being met, but we shall look at that in more detail in the chapter on the law.

The taking of the brown hare with running dogs such as Bedlington lurchers is now illegal in the UK. Pre ban though Bedlington-blooded lurchers caught brown and blue hares, and the cross that excelled was the Bedlington/greyhound, especially the three-quarter variation (Bedlington × greyhound × greyhound). The ever popular Bedlington × whippet hybrid also occasionally caught the odd hare, though to be fair these were either kicked up underfoot (meaning the animal didn't stand a chance and was taken practically in its seat or form), or taken in a spot lamp (lamping). Indeed I had a Bedlington × whippet, a large specimen for such a cross standing twenty-one inches at the shoulder, that took quite a haul of hare way back in those heady pre-ban days.

Nowadays the Bedlington × whippet has never been more popular, and I believe this is a popularity that is brought about because of the current hunting with dogs laws in the UK. Indeed a lot of money can be made by anyone who wants to breed the Bedlington × whippet for there is no denying it is a very endearing cross, very even and true to type – always, but always rough coated, and usually blue/black in colour, occasionally red or chocolate/liver and now and again brindle.

On the subject of brindle colouring I have naturally put this down to whippet being in the cross, though there are reports now, albeit hushed up, of so-called brindled pure-bred Bedlingtons turning up in certain litters! Could the source of this be genetic when brindled first-crosses appear in litters of Bedlington lurchers if such a beast as a brindled Bedlington does exist? I do wonder if such allegedly brindled dogs are born brindle and turn into a faded brindle amongst the blue, as in a blue/brindle whippet, Staffordshire bull terrier or a blue/ wheaten as in a Glen of Imaal. I certainly bred a dog like this in the case of Peter Vaux's Drifter, a first-cross Bedlington × Glen of Imaal terrier.

Back to the Bedlington × whippet. Because of the current hunting laws with dogs it has become an extremely popular lurcher now that rats and rabbits are not subject to any legal restrictions. The Bedlington × whippet takes both the brown rat and humble coney with relish. The Bedlington terrier and its hybrid brethren, plus the Bedlington lurcher, will take a wide range of quarry, some of which are now forbidden whilst others are subject to exempted hunting. It is permitted to hunt various species outside of the UK but illegal in the UK itself.

There is no denying that the rabbit is probably the number one quarry for both terriers and running dogs, although that statement will have dyed in the wool working terrier men putting their heads in their hands for the rabbit requires very little in the way of courage. What it does require, however, is nose in a terrier context, not to be cover shy (again from the terrier viewpoint) and of course high prey drive, something all working dogs should have in abundance. Regarding catching rabbits with Bedlington lurchers (or any running dog for that matter) there it does take a turn, for not only does the dog need super fitness (especially for night work) but also a certain amount of bravery and courage for that extra bit of bottomless guts when the muscles are aching and fatigue starts to set in, and here a certain amount of indomitable spirit starts to manifest itself in a good fit working dog.

So rabbit catching with dogs takes on several differing roles. We have terriers, both Bedlingtons and Bedlington hybrids, that will be used as ferreting dogs, that is to say be used for marking up occupied rabbit warrens, holding rabbits in nets long enough until the ferreter gets to the enmeshed rabbit. They also will catch an odd rabbit as it makes a mistake in close proximity to the warren or cover, or maybe just a rabbit escaping a long net.

Bedlington terriers will also work dense cover, and it is here that most Bedlingtons have success in catching healthy adult rabbits in the daylight much in the same vein as any other type of terrier. Rabbit catching in rough cover is great fun but there can often be nothing to take home at the end of the day, nevertheless every rabbit taken will be well earned and remembered forever.

Several years ago I worked a mixed pack of Bedlington-blooded lurchers, a whippet and working-strain Bedlingtons. My pack worked together brilliantly: it was like a mini pack of hounds or maybe reminiscent of a medieval hound pack when several differing types came together in one unit rather like a foxhound or beagle pack. On one

A reliable working Bedlington belonging to Matej Hraško.

hand I had my rough-cover workers, some of these terriers being bayers on rabbit whilst others were as mute as could be, these usually being the fox dogs of pre-ban days. My whippet, a blue Janice Sheridan-bred animal and my Bedlington lurchers were the catch dogs when a rabbit lost its nerve and broke cover (they really had little choice when the terriers were working the cover!), the running dogs often crashing into cover and nailing rabbits too.

If ever one needed a pointer into the Bedlington's past and its creation one need look no further than the terrier's almost hound-like 'music' or voice when it is throwing tongue and quarry is located. It is truly reminiscent of a scent hound; but here I must digress slightly. The Bedlington's past is still shrouded in mystery though it has been discussed in great length in my book *The Working Bedlington* and in

Ken Bounden's book *The Bedlington Terrier*. As this is a book about the terriers' work in the field, I don't intend to cover old ground on ancestry but will say I believe a small scent hound of otterhound type may have been introduced. Not only this, but there is a school of thought that prototype Bedlingtons or Rothbury terriers had a rough, shaggy coat rather than the linty type of coat widely associated with the dogs that assumed the name Bedlington terrier. One thing we can be sure of is that the dogs that created the breed were very closely related, for even in the early days of the Bedlington travel in Northumberland would have been tricky at least on old farm tracks in sometimes hostile terrain (hostile in the sense that winters in Northumberland would have been snowy, icy and often windy, cold and wet). Breeders or sportsmen would not have wanted to journey far to line an in-season

A Bedlington
bitch retrieves
a shot mallard
from water.

96

bitch. It is possible that some kind of aquatic scent hound may have been used in the early part of the breed's creation. Even to this day the breed displays a liking for working in water, has a great nose on it, a distinctive throaty hound-like bay and also works well in a pack environment.

It is all these qualities that make the Bedlington pack work well together in a rabbit-hunting unit. In my own small pack I had finders, hunters that kept up pressure and great catch dogs, plus of course the running dogs. Many memorable hunts ensued using this informal and relaxed style of hunting, not only that but occasional pre-ban fox and hare were taken or if we were really lucky pheasant, partridge or mallard.

Lesley Caines of the Midland Bedlington Terrier Club showed me pictures of a dog she bred and sold to a enthusiast in the USA who follows lure coursing in the States. Speedy as the Bedlington or Bedlington cross-breds might be, it never was a coursing dog, and a catcher of healthy adult rabbits in daytime it certainly was not! Recently at a Bedlington Terrier Association event near Banbury in Oxfordshire I was talking to a lady who claimed her Bedlington caught healthy adult rabbits on the run in broad daylight, and from this state-ment alone I deduced she didn't really have a clue and certainly never worked her terrier to rabbits. Animals infected by myxomatosis, young foolish rabbits or healthy rabbits in cover are a different kettle of fish.

The Bedlington terrier is certainly no slouch as terriers go; on the contrary it is possibly the fastest running terrier, though surprisingly enough Staffordshire bull terriers, the leggy fit types at least, may well run them a close second. Welsh Bedlington aficionado Steve Richards owns possibly the fastest Bedlington that I know, and when I first saw the dog it was ten years old. Amazing when one considers that even at that age it was incredibly fast for a pure-bred Bedlington. For this reason and the fact that litter wastage is never encountered, the Bedlington makes for an ideal dog to use as a lurcher base. It is here in the rabbit-catching game that Bedlington blood really comes into its own. The Bedlington lurcher can perform all the tasks that a Bedlington terrier can plus it must be admitted that little bit more, namely it will catch rabbits on the run and pre ban also the occasional hare.

Matej Hraško with his Bedlington and hare in Slovakia.

Bedlington-blooded lurchers usually inherit the Bedlington quality of good olfactory sense for which the terrier is famous. It was George Newcombe of Rillington fame that said 'a terrier is only as good as its nose' and that is very true. That quality is usually apparent in the Bedlington lurcher in both the whippet and greyhound versions and not only in the first crosses either but in three-quarter and five-eighths-bred dogs too. I bred and worked a fantastic sandy and tan smooth-coated dog that was roughly five-eighths running dog (both whippet and greyhound blood) and three-eighths Bedlington terrier. The bitch was bred down from my old Blue's line and I had worked the strain, for strain it had become having bred four generations, all the time only introducing strong racing and pre-ban coursing blood plus working-strain Bedlington terrier. The lurcher was called Goldie and had an incredible nose, stamina and early pace. I could slip Goldie on silly slips and she would still catch rabbits, frequently eating up the distance between her and them, sometimes with comparative ease. At the time I was probably lamping Goldie under favourable moonless and partly moonless nights four or five times a week, often alternating her with her dam and a tiny slip of a rough-coated bitch called Rush, and often in conjunction with a shotgun. Goldie worked happily in the presence of guns, so much so that I could work her around Bonfire Night when there were lots of bangs and pops from the fireworks.

During her working career there must have been many rabbits she caught that I will have forgotten – on the lamp that is. Daylight was a different thing. I remember one afternoon during early autumn I had taken Goldie for a walk round one of my favourite farms and at the side of a farm track adjacent to the first rut into the field Goldie stopped, savouring the strong scent that clearly must have been there, and from her excited manner I could tell there had been fair game there recently. Next day on the same route I noticed the same reaction at exactly the same spot, and this time she nosed out a large adult buck rabbit from underneath an overhanging dry thistle, pushed out her quarry very cleverly into the field and power ran it down. It was a perfect catch and one that sticks clearly in my mind; I guess everyone has a few of them in their head. Daytime rabbits are always memorable.

Goldie's grand dam, a bitch I worked purely in the daytime, was a red fawn, pretty rough lurcher called Belle. One day the Bedlingtons had worked long and hard on an experienced and well-run rabbit, when it eventually made a run for it. Belle ran it right past me, the bitch right on its tail, when I saw it stumble a bit in flight, regain its footing only to get caught within a pace or two. Belle returned the rabbit to hand and it was only when I walked down the field I noticed its tail in the grass and glancing at our prize saw she had taken its tail clean off before nailing it. I am sure that this is what has happened when we catch tail-less rabbits – either a dog or fox has amputated the tail without the benefit of anaesthetic.

So to conclude, for daytime work on rabbits make sure your dogs are stock and ferret broken and well-enough trained to return back to call. You can have fantastic fun chasing rabbits all the year round but due to the so-called growing season of the warmer months it can be more spectacular during the autumn and winter.

Alert! An outcrossed dog belonging to Chris Mulreidy.

Ferreting depends very much on the hunter. Certain folk will not tolerate a dog grabbing a netted rabbit, but personally I don't mind that and if the dog gets there before I do I will not worry for it is a rabbit in the bag. The best dogs can be worked off the lead but certain dogs sometimes never learn the knack – it depends on how excitable the dog is, how often it gets the opportunity to get out and to a degree how good and patient a trainer you are at the end of the day. Great ferreting dogs are a treasure to own and certainly never offered up for sale.

For sheer numbers of regular rabbits however one must pursue them after dark, and whilst some hunters may still use long nets, or occasionally gate nets, a vast majority of nocturnal rabbit catchers simply use the aid of a spot lamp and a lurcher. This is one area where a Bedlington will catch healthy rabbits on the run, for a clever lamp operator can certainly enhance the chances of nailing a nighttime bunny, and whilst I personally like very fast dogs (my current lamping dog at the time of writing is a pure-bred whippet, for no dog beats this breed in the speed and nimbleness stakes over fifty yards), quickness alone does not make for an efficient lamp dog. I have seen dogs literally walk down the outside of a beam and pick up a squatting rabbit before it knows what is happening. Anticipation of what the quarry is likely to do is also a quality that only comes about as a result of regular experience in the field, and by regular I don't mean once a month.

When does one enter a young dog to lamping or work at all for that matter? Coincidentally this very subject surfaced only a relatively short time ago on an internet forum I sometimes use. Various breeds take different times to work as it depends on temperament, build and of course quarry. As we are addressing the rabbit at the moment we shall endeavour to break down the pros and cons of correct entering, early entering and late entering to this species.

Certain breeds will enter to rabbit very early on, but the practice can also literally ruin a young dog, the end result being an unconfident sapling that believes it cannot possibly catch running prey at night or, sin of sins, starts to open up when in pursuit of its quarry. Terrier-blooded or whippet-based stock are often blamed for this irritating manifestation, but I personally have not found this to be the case and I have had some excellent lamp dogs of this type catching at an early age. In some cases it can be down to rubbish lamping on the part of the operator or just plain silly slips on practically uncatchable rabbits. Either way frustration often causes the fault known as giving tongue. It was a monumental fault of the poacher's dog of old, giving away the offender's presence and alerting landowner and gamekeeper alike. However I feel the real fault lies in the fact that if it is throwing tongue the pursuing dog is not breathing correctly and therefore not running to its full potential. Early entering can cause this fault.

One of the best lamp dogs I ever had was the aforementioned Goldie who caught a rabbit at the tender age of fifteen weeks. That rabbit was three parts grown and had been clipped by a discharge of number five shot from a 12 gauge shotgun, but it recovered enough to give the babe a course and a catch, and from there on in Goldie was wed to rabbit and the discharge of the old barking iron! Early entering never hurt Goldie – she made twenty-three inches at the shoulder and was a very muscular lurcher.

Conversely, another good Bedlington-bred lurcher I had was Goldie's son, a rough-coated liver dog called Leo. Leo's training went very differently. He was bred by me shortly before my divorce and consequently because of the turmoil I only had time to exercise him and precious little else. Divorces can be not only expensive but somewhat time-consuming too. When everything was sorted and an air of normality returned to our life, I started to try Leo out on the lamp. At this time he was around two years of age and had been worked daytime with my son Dale, walking the dog every day on a small piece of local permission. The dog had grown up and fully matured but not been pushed, and the first night out on difficult ground he came very close to catching. The night was mild and still. The next night couldn't have been more different, dark as could be with a howling gale, but first slip, first catch with a perfect live retrieve, and from there on Leo never looked back.

Certain breeds can take early entering whilst others cannot. Take the deerhound for example; it would be foolish to enter a dog that was underdeveloped physically, putting stress on joints, tendons and ligaments. While at the other end of the spectrum another sight hound breed, the whippet, is much more forgiving and therefore able to withstand the rigours of early entering.

Jude, my current lamping dog, was just a little over eight months old when he caught his first adult healthy rabbit on the beam. I hasten to add that this was his fourth rabbit by then, already having taken two diseased adults and a tiny rabbit that was as diminutive and green as he was at just ten weeks of age – a freak catch that wasn't expected, much less engineered. What it did do is wed the whippet firmly to rabbit. With some breeds you can get away with early entering, others not so. Physically and mentally some are just not prepared, and it's as simple as that. The lamper should bear in mind many dogs have been ruined by early entering but I have yet to hear of one that has been ruined by late entering.

Another topic worthy of examination is whether it's best to start a rabbiting dog on the beam first or perhaps start with daytime work. I actually like to use a dog first and foremost on the lamp because it teaches hunting up in the dark when prey has been missed. In many cases dogs that are used to seeing rabbits disappear into cover during daylight hours hunt on by using their noses. I dislike lamp dogs dropping their noses to the ground and refusing to return to hand, for the very good reason another catchable rabbit can be close and viable to run with possible success. You need to be able to recall a lamp dog instantly. My own personal preference is to lamp the dog first and enter it gradually from about ten months of age.

We have already established that not only does the Bedlington lurcher catch rabbits on the lamp but the pure-bred Bedlington can become adept at taking rabbits at night with the aid of a spot lamp. There are ways this possibility can be enhanced somewhat and one of these ways is taking the dog out with a marksman. This can be either with a shotgun or a rimfire rifle such as a .22 or .177 bullet gun. Invariably at some stage a rabbit will be clipped and slowed up somewhat, and for the youngster this will be a confidence booster and give the sapling much confidence and self-belief. As the dog develops it will also jell together with this gun/lurcher combination and the duo can be deadly. Here is how it works. Rabbits killed cleanly will drive a pup into a frenzy, keen and eager to catch for itself, which it does by watching the lamp, so that injured rabbits are caught easily and rabbits not shot at may present the pup with a good chance of a catch. It works equally well with an experienced dog as well. Pure-bred Bedlingtons excel at this game too.

Large bags of rabbits can be achieved by lamping.

Of course various stringent guidelines need to be adhered to and these all have to do with safety. Number one, the marksman never fires if the dog is off slip; number two, always work the dog on a slip; number three, only slip the dog when you are certain there is no hope of a shot – this may result in some rabbits getting away but this is the downside of gun/dog combos. Done correctly it is an awesome way of catching good numbers of rabbits.

All lamping dogs should retrieve rabbits back to hand so therefore this quality should be apparent in all hunting dogs, but most dogs will do this quite naturally. One of the saddest sights in lamping is a big guy thundering across a field to grab his rabbit because he thinks his dog will either let it go or run off with it. All rabbit dogs need to retrieve, day or night. The person behind the lamp should certainly give the dog a sporting chance on its rabbit but despite the fact that lamping is both effective and simple some folk just don't seem to be able to manage it properly. A few basic pointers may be of benefit.

We can use both Bedlingtons and Bedlington lurchers (or indeed any sight hound for that matter). The science behind lamping is extremely easy to understand, but despite this some folk still get it wrong. Lamping kits are easily bought nowadays at reasonable prices, and the one I would recommend is a one million candle power lamp with appropriate battery power to carry you through the session.

When to lamp? This should be on the darkest of nights with no or little moon, and the night should ideally be squally with intermittent rain. That may be the lamper's ideal, and they do happen, though sometimes it can be anything but and yet still produce. So there we have our picture: the darkest of nights, a fully charged battery, a one million candle power lamp (fitted with a filter), a nice field of newly growing wheat. The ground is soft, it's early season so our rabbits are 'green'– this year's young adults, so not yet lamp shy but big enough for the eating, prime for the taking and great for a young Bedlington or lurcher. The idea is always to get between the feeding rabbit and its escape, whether it is wood, hedgerow or maybe just a bank full of holes. Rabbits will feed out well in fields under the cover of darkness, feeling secure under the night's cover. This is totally unlike daytime rabbiting where conies stay close to the safety of cover.

There has always been some controversy and difference of opinion as to what time to venture out with dog and lamp. A lot of lampers advocate the midnight meet. This probably comes about from poaching, however when the lamper has permission the midnight meet seems nothing short of lunacy for by that time the hunter and his dog can be warmly tucked up in bed and kennel. Indeed I have caught rabbits on the lamp with a dog before it's struck 5 o'clock in the afternoon mid-winter. The twilight and eventual darkness gives the conies a lot of confidence to feed abroad and feel safe enough to venture out much further than they would normally do in daylight.

The lamp operator should approach with the wind preferably in his/her face. The idea then is possibly very obvious. You need to cut off the rabbit's escape route. Let's draw a picture: you enter a field with the wind preferably blowing into your face, because not only does this mask scent but also footfall and approach. Say a wood is to your left, so you lamp out into a field of newly sown wheat. You cast the beam in a fan shape, or semi-circle if you like, trying to locate prey. An obvious rabbit out a good way is sometimes best, but there may be a closer one nearer the edge of the field. If there's enough room for you to cut this off, that may well be your rabbit provided it stays put. This calls for some stealth, but what you should not do is switch your lamp off and this applies in any approach. Rabbits often run off hedges etc. and run up and down boundaries, and dogs often wear down and panic such quarry and thereby catch it.

Glare from your lamp is all important – I learned this when lamping foxes both when shooting and taking them with running dogs pre ban. You drop your beam to the side of the rabbit but watch it in the glare, and always work the dog on a slip as you will be moving quite suddenly and you will not reasonably have time to instruct the dog. It just won't happen. Approach your rabbit if it moves and gets up, OK full on beam on the quarry and slip the dog. Often the rabbit will stay put but if it moves drop your lamp away from it, in other words nearer the escape route but still watch in the glare. Ideally get as close as possible with the rabbit straight in front of you – it will move left or right or may run straight to you, but you must be by now lamping full on the rabbit. Rabbits squatting to evade detection sometimes move an ear or shuffle, and your dog will leave you in no doubt of this, though a novice dog may still not see it, which is very irritating when a sapling runs straight over its potential prey and that prey gets away. Gift horses should never be looked in the mouth springs to mind!

As a lamper I often move with the rabbit running sometimes hoping to cut it off, but beware fields are often uneven and you can come to grief, so weigh up that situation. However by doing this and rocking the lamp (strobing) you will be amazed how many rabbits do get caught. With time and experience dogs soon realise that the rabbit that hits cover often just stops, thinking it is safe, which is not so once a dog realises this and follows it in. Very often you will catch a rabbit in this way, out of the light's beam.

Filters are important. I always use them, very rarely do I rely on the bright white beam. There are many different colours to choose. I have mine but I say to you, try the colours and just use which one you find best.

Dogs should come back immediately, either with caught prey or when they miss put them back on slip and ready to go again. I always use slips. As to the type, well personally I actually don't know anyone ever to use the shop-sold coursing slips. What I use is a very soft slim piece of rope, which does not dig in and is very comfortable. Lamping dogs should retrieve and hopefully bring everything to hand alive.

Rabbits should be dispatched quickly and as humanely as possible. This is best achieved by holding the prey firmly by the back legs and the neck held between the middle and index finger of your other hand. Pull and push with your hands at the same time, and you will feel the neck break. The dispatch is instant and as humane as you can possibly make it be.

The rat is public health enemy number one, disease ridden, despised and persecuted by all. In essence it is a highly intelligent and sophisticated animal with a complex social order, one of the natural world's greatest survivors and a fantastic quarry species worthy of pursuit by working terriers.

Traditionally the brown rat (*Rattus norvegicus*) was pursued by terriers and men in conjunction with ferrets, but in recent times this has become less popular as firstly the exhaust of chainsaws made to run too rich and of late commercially produced smokers manufactured with rat control in mind have come into play. Stopping up escape routes within pigsties and battery pens before a hunt and then throwing

Rother's Ratters, Steve Richard's and Chris Mulreidy's dogs get down to business on rats with a little bit of help from a Jack Russell.

the light switches on as the terriers enter is also a tried and tested way of catching rats. You can also lamp rats in and around farm yards with Bedlingtons, and Bedlington/whippet hybrids often excel at this.

Hunting rats when a farmer is clearing out his yard is also good fun using motley bands of canines, from terriers, running dogs, mongrels and collies joining in, while the odd farm cat has been known to put in an appearance. It's generally a case of straw bales or farm equipment being moved and rodents bolting, and if you don't know what the 'rat dance' is watch a big man with a pitchfork and a determined rat evading capture. It's a bit of a jig believe me!

Bolting rats with ferrets is still practised but it's a dying art as more and more people opt for the more efficient and less messy or risky method of smoking out. Commercially available smokers that pump smoke down the rat warren result in big bags of rats especially after the shooting season has ended in February and the rodents are feeding frenziedly on the game birds' feed. Warrens are usually encountered around the pheasant feeders and one hundred plus bags of rodents are not uncommon. It's a quick and easy way of getting rats to bolt for terriers and does away with the sometimes messy and dangerous ferreting of rats where the rodents were bolted to dogs or sometimes into delicate rat nets which are rather like a diminutive purse net.

Rats bite with great fury and inflict incredible pain, so all terriers to be used in ratting need to be inoculated against the rat catcher's yellows, the dreaded Weil's disease or leptospirosis. Though it must be said I think working terriers used for this do build up a natural immunity to the disease over a period of time – just my opinion, I hasten to add. Most terriers will kill rats and I personally have caught thousands of the critters with several different types of dogs: whippets, greyhounds, lurchers, collies, Lakeland, Jack Russell, Manchester, Glen of Imaal, Staffordshire bull terriers and of course Bedlington terriers.

My Bedlingtons when kennelled outside would explode with excitement if they heard a Fenn trap or the clink of a rat cage go off, for even working dogs sometimes attract rats, would you believe, as sure as any chicken or pigeon loft, I'm afraid. Frequently I would find a Bedlington lying on a dead rat caught as it made its way across a run. I was loath to poison with dogs around, preferring to trap and let the dogs catch. This, coupled with the fact I hunted rats for fun made my Bedlingtons dynamite rat hunters. Bedlington terriers make good ratting terriers, there is no doubt of this.

I used to run a small pack to rats along a dirty polluted stream that once held watercress but at the time held only raw sewage and discarded sanitary towels and condoms. It was a vile place and one even I stopped hunting after the lurcher dived in after a rat thinking it was terra firma only to find it was an evil green slick. I decided enough was enough and gave up hunting the filthy brook for more pleasant pastures. The lot of a rat hunter can be hunting in unpleasant places at the best of times, but I decided not all of the time.

Wales has always had a massive interest in working Bedlingtons, and it still does, but between the two World Wars Welsh miners often ratted (and dug badger) with their dogs. Many of these dogs were out and out working Bedlingtons, though hybrids between this breed and Staffordshire bull terriers were not unknown. D.B. Plummer in his *Rogues and Running Dogs* writes of such dogs allegedly entering into

An Eakring ratting Bedlington of John Piggin's breeding. As a rodent operative, John worked his dogs daily.

the predominantly white-bodied 'Russell-type dogs', that were so popular in South Wales at the time. I also often wonder if the Sealyham terrier has any genetic links to the Bedlington. Certainly, Jack Russell/Bedlington hybrids are not unknown; I know one owned by Leon Robinson of Milton Keynes. The dog is a good all-round terrier but one which is dynamite on rats bolted by the smoker.

Generally speaking Bedlingtons take to rat hunting like ducks do to water; it is a completely natural quarry and one worthy of pursuit. In my experience, terriers that kill rats use two different methods of dispatch: the first is a great way of fast finish; and the second is the grab, shake and drop, the method used by a lot of Jack Russells and the king of the rat pits – the Manchester terrier. Generally speaking Bedlingtons don't kill this way, they simply grab and bite. It's a ferocious hard bite, reminiscent of a Staffordshire bull terrier. The fact that Bedlingtons generally work well with ferrets makes for a terrier that will do an efficient job in the traditional role of ferret/terrier in pursuit of rats. The Bedlington fulfils an excellent role when used with a smoker and large numbers of rats are on the cards. All in all the working Bedlington is a rat hunter par excellence.

In a world where we accept that grey squirrels are a major pest some may find it hard to believe that killing one with a dog in the UK is illegal, but it is! You can shoot one, trap one but urge your dog on one and you are a criminal. Back in time when it was legal, Bedlingtons made stunning grey squirrel dogs, being hard bitten and fleet of foot. Much the same applies when it comes to mink, weasels and stoat. The current law states that you cannot kill with a dog but you can shoot or trap; you can't kill a hare with a dog but you can fly a hawk…. Thus is life I'm afraid.

Essentially the Bedlington is an earth dog, a true terrier, one that went to ground, the fox being its traditional quarry, but then again before legislation so was the piggy-eyed black-and-white, Bloody Bill Brock, the badger. But before we look at these most traditional quarries we shall look at the last few miscellaneous tasks placed before Bedlingtons in the field.

Hunting hares with dogs may be illegal now in the UK, yet back in the day even Bedlington terriers were sometimes used on this the most testing of sporting quarry. Hares were worked in the same manner as by a beagle or basset pack. The brown hare is one of Mother Nature's major miracles, a beast of rebirth, the original Easter bunny, a beast of mythical properties and folklore adored by the Celtic peoples of Britain until the Vikings arrived with their blood lust and cravings (though to be fair the Romans hunted *Lepus capensis* with great relish as did their beagle-type hounds) and slew the long-eared one with as much enthusiasm as they did the boar and hart.

Its entire existence encompasses all that is raw in the fields from the rumbling of the combines to the sly vixen who needs the leverets' bowels and flesh to sustain her growing, demanding and boisterous litter of cubs. It is a life full of perils, an existence with an eye on staying alive. Thus is the life of the brown hare. Maddy Prior, the one-time lead vocalist of the folk/rock band Steeleye Span recorded a song called 'The Hare' which absolutely epitomises the life of this, one of Mother Nature's major, major miracles.

The hare was *the* ultimate test for any coursing dog pre ban, though their slower cousins the scent hounds like Bedlington terriers (a related breed in one form or another) ran down the lagomorph in a war of attrition that often encompassed many moments and indeed many fields. Suffice to say that hares, both the brown and 'blue' mountain hare, were a test on any hunting dog pre ban though it must be conceded that the brown was more highly revered than its smaller blue cousin.

111

I recently corresponded with someone who used to work pre-ban hares with a small pack of Bedlington/beagle hybrids, mainly black and tan, blue grizzle and tri-coloured composites. Sadly no pictures were left of his dogs but he rated this hybrid for its dense coat, robust hybrid constitution, fantastic nose and undying gameness and stamina when in pursuit of quarry. His pack was but eight couple, nonetheless they accounted for many pre-ban hare and the occasional fox. George Newcombe made mention of a Bedlington a friend of his had, a small bitch that used to grab hares in their seats, and although often towed away by the hare, yet still the somewhat small Bedlington hung on to her prize. Newcombe also mentioned another that wore down hares in a beagle-type fashion.

Obviously at the time of writing we can only write of work at the hare, be it either the brown or blue mountain hare, in a historical context. Hares were run with Bedlingtons by scent and then chased, and although few were caught some were flushed, coursed and caught with sight hounds. Which brings me nicely to a point: hares have been coursed successfully by Bedlington-bred lurchers both day and night.

Lamping hares was remarkably easy with sight hounds, either pure bred or Bedlington bred, and a star's flight away from coursing under rules where the wild brown hare was afforded fair law, for lamping hares pre ban was a fairly easy task for even some mediocre running dogs. That said there always was the odd old hare that had seen it all before, been run and lived to tell the tale so to speak. Lamp-shy hares or hares that knew the way of running dogs coming at them from out of the dark often gave great accounts of themselves to the point that many lamping men out for numbers of rabbits on a night on the beam would gladly turn off the switch of their lamp in preference to catching the humble coney. The exertion spent on the catching of one hare was often compared to the catching of twenty rabbits on the beam, if you had a wily old hare in front of your dog that is!

Leverets just after the corn was cut that suddenly found themselves in a barren, open landscape post-combine harvester were easy meat for mini lurchers such as Bedlington × whippets or even the most heavily built collie lurcher. If heavily built collie lurchers caught the occasional pre-ban hare then the long-eared one also occasionally fell to the jaws of the working Bedlington on the lamp.

Hares on the lamp? Well if you got a wily one pre ban maybe it would give you the run around but if you got a 'green' one they were remarkably easy for they run back towards the lamper and often as not up and down hedgerows, falling to the dog as it enters cover, stopping and getting caught. Many years ago and, thus pre ban of course, I entered a field where I had permission with a diminutive nineteen-inch rough-coated Bedlington-bred lurcher, when my Coleman half-million candle power lamp picked up a pair of red eyes. Thinking it to be a rabbit I walked up my quarry, whereupon it exploded into life. I slipped my bitch yards away from this large hare and within a few yards she had caught it. It kicked like mad, eventually freeing itself, screaming as it did and thus a nighttime course began. That hare ran my bitch ragged in that field on that windy, dark night. The brown hare is a super fit, brilliant miracle of Mother Nature's creation and should always, but always, be given our upmost respect.

To be fair the taking of hares with Bedlington-blooded stock has always been the prerogative of the lurcher (by which I mean greyhound rather whippet bred). First-cross Bedlington/greyhound hybrids were capable enough takers of the occasional hare but it was to the three-quarter greyhound, quarter Bedlington terrier that one looked for a decent show on a hare. It was dogs thus bred that although unfashionable amongst the pre-ban hare-coursing fraternity in general were employed by daytime coursing folk. Hares in general were not regarded perhaps as the traditional quarry of the Bedlington terrier pre ban, but their hybrid running dog kin certainly did give a good account of themselves on the wild brown hare.

Gary Taylor, a hunter from Markfield, had two first-cross Bedlington/greyhound hybrids that I bred that not only coursed and caught hares but also accounted for pre-ban fox too. Before I take a close look at the true role of any terrier, namely an earth dog, I will look at some of the lesser more obscure uses of Bedlingtons in the field, for the working Bedlington has long been recognised as the terrier that will perform well in a wide range of tasks.

John Piggin used his Eakring-bred dogs in a wide variety of circumstances from not only traditional terrier work but also at shoots. Lady Lena of Eakring was just one of John's dogs that was used alongside the spaniels and Labradors picking up on pheasant shoots. I have used

The legendary Floyd of Eakring was never the best coated of dogs but one which bestowed good shape and balance on his progeny. Owned by the Newark rat catcher John Piggin.

Bedlingtons for picking up myself game shooting, pigeon shooting and wildfowling, and it was at the latter my Bedlingtons excelled. I have had terriers swim out and retrieve both ducks and geese off the water; no mean feat by any standards.

Pre-ban mink were hunted by packs of Bedlingtons, again because their natural liking of water made the Bedlington an ideal aquatic dog and, before it was declared illegal, the otter was also hunted with Bedlingtons. This was a savage adversary, as old accounts of otter hunting readily testify.

Also back in time when it was legal there are many tales concerning Bedlingtons being used on deer; indeed there are still some stalkers to this day who use Bedlingtons to track wounded deer including beasts as big as sika and red deer, but it was on the diminutive but stocky and aggressive muntjac deer that the breed excelled.

Muntjac, or 'munty' as the species is affectionately called, are powerful beasts when threatened and males or bucks fight with great fury with not only their tusks but also their small antlers. With powerful necks and an almost pig-like physique the barking deer of India could inflict severe damage on small and finely built dogs. Indeed even bigger more powerful lurchers such as collie crosses have come to grief from the tusks of the cornered muntjac.

Muntjac deer, like the Chinese water deer, are escapees from properties that now suffer crop and shrub damage due to this fascinating small deer. For all its doggedness muntjac pre ban fell prey to Bedlingtons. Particularly the bigger dogs and Bedlington lurchers were dynamite on the munty. Speaking of Bedlington lurchers not only did they wed well to muntjac but also roe and even fully grown fallow were brought to book pre ban with Bedlington-blooded lurchers.

There was one story of a genuine three-quarter-bred sight hound, quarter Bedlington (sire working saluki, dam Bedlington/greyhound) who coursed and caught a large muntjac buck, its owner running in and dispatching the stricken deer with a fatal cut of his knife to the throat. The catch had happened at the back of a water board sewerage works allegedly near a town centre. With no way of getting the catch back the hunter had gralloched his prize, hung it in a nearby tree and trudged home, returning back to the point of kill minus his dog but with a hessian sack. The kill was enveloped therein and the hunter carried it across his shoulders to a nearby waiting taxi rank, where the cab driver allegedly said 'Looks heavy son, what you got there?' to which the lurcher man replied 'Oh just a deer' and the laughing unsuspecting driver took him home – or so the story goes!

Nowadays things are so much different and any owners of either Bedlington lurchers or Bedlington terriers should be aware that even a casual walk in the countryside can be

Bedlingtons are great trackers of game including large quarry such as red or sika deer.

fraught with potential problems which could ultimately bring trouble and even the confiscation of your dog(s). A recent incident was brought to my attention concerning a brace of running dogs on an evening walk. A muntjac was chased and caught by a dog out of sight. Well, firstly dogs in the countryside must be kept under strict control and clearly here the dogs were out of sight for some time. Eventually the owners caught up with the dogs, one of which had hold of a doe muntjac. At this point, because it is forbidden to course deer with dogs, attempts should have been made to get the dogs off, but instead our hunter raced to a nearby vehicle to get his shotgun! A shotgun left unattended in an empty car is one thing and the use of a weapon not legally allowed to shoot deer is another! The fact he had time to get to the vehicle, get the gun, get back and take a shot that would not kill his dog proves to my mind that he ultimately had time and was proficient enough to get his dog off forbidden quarry and his energies should have been expended on keeping within the law. Presumably the owner was capable of getting the dog off as I don't think anyone would be stupid enough to fire at a dog locked on to a deer. The deer was allegedly dispatched illegally by a shotgun. Pictures said to be of the scene showed a gassed-up ungralloched dead muntjac with a cut throat!

The reader can see a catalogue of errors, misdemeanours and down-right illegal activities; accidental catch or not such actions by owners of working terriers or running dogs bring legitimate lurcher and terrier work into disrepute and provide ammunition to those who seek an end to all dog work, and ultimately field sports in general. Posting such actions and pictures on internet websites is quite another matter, and a half-decent prosecution would make a meal of such an action. I am sure such hunters would ponder their actions with a sad and heavy heart as their gun licences would probably be revoked, they could get a criminal record and have their much loved dogs confiscated. Believe me such things can happen!

It's not just Bedlington lurchers who catch and hold deer, however. Pure-bred and hybrid terriers too have been used in the past on cloven-hoofed quarry. Big Bedlingtons (there have always been large Bedlingtons) have been useful on larger more powerful quarry, whether it's pre-ban fox or even before legislation made it illegal, the Furry Humbug himself, Bloody Bill Brock the badger.

Badger hunting in Europe. Traditionally the badger was dug extensively by early north of England sportsmen and terriers including of course the Bedlington, back in the day when it was still legal.

Bedlington terriers wed well especially to muntjac deer as did their hybrid kin. Bedlington × Staffords were according to somewhat sketchy reports adept at finding, fixing and holding the small barking deer of India, despite the fighting reputation of this albeit small but nonetheless powerful adversary. Many dogs, both lurchers and terriers, have come to grief over the slashing and bloody doggedness of the fighting muntjac; shoulders have been ripped to the bone by this rather sturdy deer. Yes, the muntjac is small, pig-like and tough beyond belief, except in the eating, for it is the finest of venison.

The hunting of any deer with a dog is illegal, but tracking it as wounded game, that is to say when a deer is wounded by a rifle, becomes acceptable with a dog as it is with a hare. A minefield or what! There is a stalker in Scotland who uses a Bedlington to track wounded deer, and he finds them satisfactory. As we know the breed is legendary for its olfactory sense so would be great used for this purpose.

The Bedlington worked within a pack environment and worked well in a unit, when the taking of deer was legal (pre ban); in fact it was something the breed was used to as I believe early large Bedlingtons were used as catch dogs in and around the English/ Scottish borders in a time when the breed was used for a hound/lurcher type of hunting and the quarry, most of it illegal now, would have been of a heavier type and therefore more dangerous. Not only were roe taken but also foxes, otters, martens and polecats and the last of the English wildcats. Roe deer were easier prey for Bedlingtons and Bedlington lurchers than ironically the smaller muntjac.

Hunters of deer all recognised the need to gralloch the catches immediately and certainly within twenty minutes of dispatch. Whether it was pre ban or the taking of deer with the use of a big centrefire such as a .243 rifle, the preparation of the kill was paramount. (It also shows some respect for the dignity of the quarry.) Deer were usually hung in a tree and left for five to ten minutes, then it was advocated pressing the chest diaphragm fairly hard and vigorously for around a dozen or so times, so the blood would be voided by a throat cut or decapitation after the intestines had been removed. The gassing up of deer accelerates in warmer conditions when the carcass takes longer to cool. Guts left in contaminate venison badly and taint the flesh – one good reason why it is best to remove the bowels within a short period of killing of the deer and hanging it up so nothing nasty happens, like the ruminant's stomach rupturing and voiding its messy green contents into the loins thereby ruining the butchering of the deer. This is in stark contrast to those amateurs who have left the contents of the stomach in the deer.

As a footnote to butchering, all deer should be gralloched as quickly as possible just as rabbits should be gutted straight away. The hare ironically should be left to stand for twenty-four hours and then its entrails removed. (It is still legal to shoot hares and/or flush them with a dog to the shotgun, see the chapter on the law.)

It has always been illegal to take deer with dogs or rifle at night. The lamping of all deer species is highly illegal. Yet folk used to take deer with dogs on ground that they had permission on, and of course using both Bedlingtons and Bedlington lurchers to track game injured by guns is perfectly legal. I was at a show once in Leicestershire many years ago and was approached by a uniformed policeman, an on-duty spectator I presumed, who asked me about my now long-dead-and-gone Bedlington lurcher, Blue. The officer asked 'Have you done any big stuff with her?' It's not what you expect to hear from your everyday copper, is it! I replied: 'Foxes' (pre ban). His reply was direct: 'No, I mean deer. I have seen this bitch drop a full grown doe fallow,' but he added 'I know you don't, Blue,' patting the rough-coated black/blue bitch on the head. Blue was the only dog I ever had as a fully trained adult; she was given to me by a friend who in turn had acquired her initially from a friend.

Traditionally the true vocation of the terrier is that of an earth dog and the Bedlington is no different. It has always provided an alternative to the traditional working terriers, and in the area where I grew up (the Midlands) Jack Russell-type terriers reigned supreme. It was only in the late 1970s that coloured dogs started to emerge as alternative types in the Midlands and south of England with the so-called Patterdale terrier being at the forefront of this southern invasion of the northern working terrier breeds. Around this time Lakelands and Border terriers too had started to gain impetus in the popularity stakes and were beginning to win well at fell and moorland Working Terrier Club shows. Despite this enough folk were around to remember a unique type of terrier that bridged a gap almost between working terriers and running dogs, and that dog of course was the Bedlington terrier.

Southern hunters had very few dogs to go on, the true underground terrier still being most popular 'up north', but South Wales too had always been a hotbed for working Bedlington terriers. Both areas had strong working terrier heritages, the north relying very much upon a old Bedlington influence within certain strains of fell terrier and ultimately Lakelands, whilst the Welsh had always regarded a game dog as a good dog, especially when used in the days when badger digging was practised and was still perfectly legal. Both the fox and the badger were widely regarded as the real quarry of a true working terrier.

Regarding the badger, the Billy, the Brock, the Furry Humbug, there was always a difference between badger digging and badger baiting, though an awful number of folk confuse the two together. Badger work

119

Slovakian earth dog.

in the UK is now totally illegal, and without exempted hunting so is working foxes with terriers. Where a fox is proven to be taking game birds there is a loophole. Under current legislation certain criteria need to be met in order for a terrier to work underground to fox, and this I will discuss in the chapter on the law. It is called exempted hunting and it applies to hunting a brace of dogs above ground too. In very clear terms the hunting of rabbits and rats has not changed but all other pest species: grey squirrels, stoats, weasels, mink and even the house mouse, come under the same protection as the fox!

Back in pre-ban days Bedlington terriers provided an alternative to the conventional white and coloured terriers, and famous dogs ran from varied times. Famous working Bedlingtons that saw work underground to fox included Norman Stead's Spring Dancer, Margaret Williamson's Worton Demon, George Newcombe's Rillington Resolute, John Piggin's Jasper of Kentene, my own The Mad Ratter and Stuart Staley's Minkstone Maverick to name but some. John Holden's Granitor dogs are well known as pre-ban foxing dogs too.

There have been throughout the course of both the Bedlington and Bedlington-blooded lurcher's history good fox control dogs and whilst terrier work can still encompass the fox under exempted hunting there is no such loophole regarding the lamping of foxes with lurchers, for here there is no way that the intention can ever be argued that the dog is being actively encouraged not to engage its quarry, and so therefore lamping foxes with dogs is now illegal. Therefore in a historical context we will discuss the pre-ban taking of the fox with Bedlington lurchers (we can also include some outsize Bedlington terriers and hybrid terriers too).

Traditionally August is a good time to lamp foxes. Marksman still know the importance of being on freshly combined crops for all stubbles attract foxes keen to dine on all the goodies there from rodents and mutilated rabbits to an abundance of invertebrate creatures, not least worms (haven't we all heard of mousing and worming foxes?). I have a friend who moves heaven and earth to get on a freshly combined field, for he knows he will shoot lots of 'green' foxes during late July and August on the stubbles with his big centrefire rifle, squealing in the big cubs to bring the vulpines under control. The same used to go for lamping foxes with dogs pre ban. Early season foxes often came in to the squeal with remarkable ease.

Bedlington × greyhound, both first and second crosses, made efficient

Granitor dog Jimmy owned by John Holden.

121

foxing dogs and just occasionally outsize Bedlingtons were also used, and I also heard of one three-quarter whippet × Bedlington that was allegedly a competent pre-ban fox dog. Many years ago and therefore once again before the ban, I had an outsized first-cross Bedlington × whippet who absolutely 'mothered' foxes both day and night. If you were part of a shooting syndicate, did some gamekeeper work for the local shoot, shot foxes yourself or went out with a pre-ban terrier and lurcher pack, chances are that your dog would find its entering to fox quite easy – nothing encourages a sapling or rookie youngster more than watching an experienced dog doing the business! Be that as it may, most Bedlington-blooded dogs regarded foxes as 'fair game' and both ran and killed them with gusto. Occasionally one used to find dogs that didn't like the sharp end or were just reluctant to attack a fox with any conviction or determination.

Similarly there were dogs that would engage a fox, but simply made a meal of it by fighting it rather than dispatching it quickly, so for this reason small dogs made dubious choices as efficient foxing dogs. Whippet × Bedlingtons of diminutive proportions, for example sixteen to eighteen inches at the shoulder, and whippets made doubtful prospects as foxing dogs, and whilst there are numerous accounts of foxes being killed by whippets in the pre-ban past (I had one) I think there was no advantage in such dogs having to take on a large dog fox for example.

Even some larger lurchers made a meal of killing a fox, for either they held back a little or just simply did not quite get the knack. Jaw to jaw locks were often prolonged, always bloody and definitely painful for both dog and fox – certainly not good, despite the fact the lurcher would come out the better, so it was not good publicity for the then pre-ban method of foxing and sometimes ended up with the dog in 'hospital'. Bedlington lurchers that hit their fox hard initially and administered the fatal throat hold, or shook the fox, finished the confrontation in double quick time. There was no denying that however good a dog was a regular foxing Bedlington lurcher did from time to time get bitten and no regular foxing dog escaped without some scar tissue.

Lamping foxes was similar to rabbit hunting with a spot lamp, in that you approach in a downward wind, the most subtle difference being sometimes you wanted the fox to know you were there (or at least that something was), perhaps encouraging the fox with a squeal. For those of you who don't realise what 'squealing' or 'calling' is I shall explain. It is the mimicking of stricken prey, a rabbit or hare maybe although some foxes 'belt in' to quieter mouse squeaks; it just depends on the fox. For all its effectiveness a fox that lives to tell the tale would be very difficult to bring in to the sight of a strong beam of light and a high-pitched squeal. Squeals can be made by putting hand to mouth and sucking back through the fingers or thumb and finger with the lips. Practice makes perfect as the saying goes and this is certainly the case with fox calling. Shop-bought calls can be purchased and they do work from time to time; it's all trial and error and possibly preference, and what you are confident with. I personally prefer calling by sucking air through the fingers, and fingers and thumbs.

Glare in lamping foxes is I believe extremely important as is a filter, but the choice of colour in the filter is down to the individual. I liked to lamp to one side of a fox, only dropping the beam down solid on the quarry when you are ready to slip or as the case is now when you are ready to shoot, for the only lamping of foxes that you can legally still do is lamping with guns or certain calibre rifles. Outsize Bedlingtons also performed well enough as lamping fox dogs pre ban much in the same way as they have with lamping rabbits from time to time. I once heard of a Bedlington × Jack Russell hybrid that was supposedly adept at catching and dealing with foxes on the lamp.

Bedlington lurchers were often used on a fox-shooting drive, and in fact they still are. Here woods and spinneys are beat and escaping foxes are shot by waiting guns with 12 gauge shotguns; sometimes foxes were shot dead and at other times they were clipped. It was here that lurchers and Bedlingtons came into play, and in a similar way to hare drives, you cannot kill one with your dog alone but your charge can trail and pick up an injured animal.

Big Bedlingtons used at night (pre ban) and sometimes on drives in the day often went on to make seizer dogs at the end of a pre-ban fox dig. This was the terrier that went in and engaged the fox at the climax of the dig and drew out the animal, similar to the situation that existed back in the time before the abolition of badger digging, where large terriers such as not only outsize Bedlingtons but other game strong breeds such as English and Stafford bull terriers and the Irish breeds were used as badger-seizing dogs.

Most Bedlington terriers show some interest in holes as do a good many terrier breeds. The old terrier books and some purists say you should work the dog only to fox, but most fox earths can be identified as just that – a fox earth, though I have known some earths or maybe warrens that hold both the fox and rabbits at the same time! There are many tales of large hob ferrets bolting fully grown foxes from what appeared to be a rabbit warren much to the surprise of the ferreters.

Dogs seeing other terriers at work quickly got the idea of what was required of them, but current legislation now decrees only a single dog is to be used in exempted hunting, so having two dogs on site may be tantamount to encouraging allegations being levelled at the terrier man which although may be untrue could be difficult to disprove. Terriers should not have been entered to fox until fully mature and have the required mental disposition to enter the inky blackness of a fox earth. I used to find that saplings encouraged to hunt rabbit, rat and to worry dead foxes that we had shot wed to the red one with no apparent problems. Foxes are very pungent animals in any case, easily smelt by human olfactory senses, so a dog finds fox scent easily. It was easier pre ban when saplings were put to ground or followed through easy earths after an experienced terrier had been through, but nonetheless most terriers wed to fox without problem.

One thing to remember is a that a terrier should not let the fox past him in a tube once he has been fixed at a particular spot, for this can be both frustrating to the terrier man or 'digger' and be very tiresome and time-consuming. Also, no working terrier, regardless of breed, should be put to ground without a locating collar fitted to the dog. There are several kinds and these will vary in price, but one thing is for certain, do not put a dog to ground on a game bird or bird killing fox unless that terrier is fitted with one of the locating devices. Both Deben and Bellman Flint are well-known, tried and tested locating devices.

To most working terrier men it wasn't a morning out unless you had a dig; I couldn't think of anything I would be less inclined to do, for I am a gardener and I dig all week so I certainly don't want to dig for fun at the weekend! If an earth is approached quietly it is possible to bolt a fox for the gun or pre ban for running dogs to take. Alternatively they could be netted much in the same way a ferreter catches a rabbit with a purse net.

George Newcombe worked many of his Rillington Bedlington and Lakeland terriers to ground on fox, especially in his early days. George often said to me: 'It was the real terrier who went to ground and bolted its fox, for a terrier is only as good as its nose.' Indeed Newcombe was extremely critical of those who sought only to dig their terrier, going on to voice concerns about the destruction of fox earths due to careless and occasionally indiscriminate digging practices. Like many old-school working terrier men Newcombe was very concerned by those individuals who blocked up fox earth entrances once a dog was to ground purely so the fox had no escape route and they could guarantee a dig.

All that said, sometimes digs were inevitable. I remember putting a dog to ground (pre ban) one freezing cold, hoar-frosted morning, the earth being an innocent one-holer from which in the past I had bolted foxes on two previous occasions when the lurchers had run Charlie to ground. On both these occasions, a Bedlington had followed it in quite unexpectedly whilst on mid-winter afternoon exercise on a small piece of permission. On both those occasions it was Rock Star, one of the best finders I have known and a bitch who had tremendous tongue. I had taken two foxes with relative ease from this earth with not even a spade or locater with me; it was quite unplanned. So imagine how I would have felt if I had known just how deep this innocent looking one-holer went. I was about to find out!

The morning in question had dawned extremely cold and frosty, after several days of severe cold weather when the daytime temperature had barely gone above freezing, but despite this the soil was unfrozen after a few inches so you could easily dig if you needed to. Snow had been forecast and with more severe night frosts imminent a friend and I had gone to help clear some pasture where the earliest pregnant ewes would shortly be brought prior to lambing. It would be good practice to keep the local fox population down to a minimum if at all possible. We had tried two earths to no avail, when we decided on the old innocent one-hole earth under a bank side. There was a clue there. Just how deep did it go in and what direction did that one entry tube take?

125

I had Rat Pit Billy with me, a blue Bedlington who was wearing a fifteen-foot locator collar on him when he entered to ground. All went quiet, really quiet; my friend waited with the 12 gauge shotgun. Nothing, shoulders were shrugged and then I decided to have a bleep about with the knocker box. To start with I thought I would find him easily but after half hour or so I was getting a little concerned. The tube went straight in but only appeared to go down slightly, and then straight into the mound behind it, where the hawthorn grew thickly. Before I could attempt locating my dog, I needed to lop this forest of hawthorn. Cold it may have been but I was down to a T-shirt and combat trousers in no time and the sweat was pouring from me.

Still no sign of the Bedlington Billy, so I went up on the hill and scanned around and got a bleep, just! At fifteen foot it is not good. We waited a little while, had a cup of coffee, went back to the same fifteen foot spot, where we netted up the entrance hole and both of us started to dig. We carried on bleeping the dog, and my friend turned to me saying: 'I hope he doesn't go deeper.' I bleeped the terrier again – gone!

We carried on re-scanning, but nothing. The morning had gone, and the afternoon had arrived, and what little bit of strength the weak winter sun still had seemed to disappear with alarming swiftness. So we dug, periodically checking to see if we could get another fix on the absent terrier. Once, just once we got a quick bleep at fifteen foot and then silence, so we dug on towards the last place we had located him. By now our spades had found thick grey clay, and anyone who has dug clay will know how heavy and hard that can be. There were no mobile phones in those days and I often wonder now how we coped. My friend suggested getting a mutual friend of ours to help us, as by now it was starting to become a blisteringly cold winter's evening. As luck would have it our friend came sauntering along towards us curious to see how we had done and why we weren't back at home by mid-afternoon cleaning out the ferrets etc.

The ewes in the distance resembled little pieces of cotton wool on the hills and despite the seriousness of the scene it also had a bleak kind of beauty. With our friend was his team of Jack Russells and a greyhound, and when we told him the tale he too set to digging the bowels of the earth.

Eventually we broke through to where Billy had last been located, but one big old hole had now been excavated and we could barely see another tube, so my two friends went to the farm cottage to get some lanterns and telephone home. My other friend took his pack home and returned with a sturdy but spannable white terrier, which obviously carried bull blood in its make up. Collared up, the bitch followed up the tube. We bleeped her another eight foot away for a fix and then set to, getting a reassuring tick-tock of two locator collars in unison. At 11pm we broke through the thick heavy grey clay as my friend's Russell pulled on a very dead cold vixen's back end dislodging the fox as she did so. When I shone the torch up the tube I could see Billy trying to get up to a dog fox on a ledge just out of his reach. Though the fox had bitten his muzzle several times, and though he was tired the terrier was encouraged by our presence and just pushed forward and locked on his fox, and from that point our dig was over. It had taken several hours and the backfilling took a couple of days, but the result was worth it. Foxing terriers need to stick at it and not let the quarry give them the run around underground, and they need to be resolute and game, but as Mr Newcombe said they are 'only as good as their nose'.

Badger work is illegal, totally illegal in the UK, but the badger was once a quarry hunted underground with terriers including Bedlingtons, and the badgers often killed or maimed their adversaries. It is true to say the only thing you can do today with a badger sett is look at it and sometimes that courts unwelcome attention too! However, some coun-tries still allow terriers to work badgers as they do fox but in Britain the badger is firmly forbidden and must be therefore left very firmly alone.

So all reference to the badger and its taking by terriers is purely in a historical context. When badger digging was considered a legitimate pastime, around the early part of the twentieth century, various badger-digging clubs sprang up. Gentlemen partook in this activity smartly dressed and a certain code of practice was put into place. It was a far cry from the pictures we sometimes see or stories that we read about in newspapers or TV news reports, where unfortunate badgers have been taken illegally from their countryside setts and ruthlessly baited with bull-blooded dogs. In fact badger baiting and badger digging have

127

always been two separate activities as different as fox digging and fox baiting. On a correctly conducted dig badgers were often dug up by terrier men completely unharmed, and sometimes even the terriers emerged unscathed. A baying dog was highly prized for in those days there were no location devices and the incessant barking always alerted the digger to the exact location; using terriers to ground invariably resulted in a dig, so a terrier that was a bayer was essential.

Other dogs were sometimes used in badger digging especially at the end of the dig. These terriers were usually big, very game, invariably mute and impervious to pain. The obvious choices were bull and terrier types, long-legged Staffords, occasional English bull terriers, wheaten terriers and just now and again a Glen of Imaal terrier, though sometimes Bedlingtons were used as well.

Undoubtedly the gamest of badger-hunting Bedlingtons were used in the creation of various types of fell terrier, these terriers almost certainly being the predecessors of the open-coated terriers known as Ullswater terriers that were bred at one time by the various Earls of Lonsdale at Lowther Castle. The earliest reference to these types of open-coated terriers is in 1732. Joe Bowman, the famous huntsman of the Ullswater pack, allegedly had a strain of rough open-coated light fawn or wheaten-coloured terriers that stayed true to that colour for at least fifty years. The open-coated blue, blue grizzles, red grizzles, blue and tans and blues had more than a passing resemblance to Bedlingtons and the story of Tommy Dobson's chocolates is a very well-known one.

Terriers of this ilk were also remarkably long backed, just like a real Bedlington, Dandie Dinmont terrier and what may or may not have been the old Rothbury terrier. Is it possible the open-coated badger hunting dogs were real Patterdale terriers, the forerunners of the Lakeland terrier, and was it that do-or-die attitude of the badger-hunting Bedlington that endeared them to early Lakeland huntsmen who required a dog to either bolt or kill its fox? Ainsley's Piper, that first Bedlington terrier, had an awesome reputation as a game dog (as did most of the prototype Rothburys or Bedlington types of the day). It is documented that at the age of just eight months he entered to badger and drew another when he was toothless at the age of fourteen years.

It is said that badgers were baited by Bedlingtons in the South Wales area, and Plummer relates the story in his *Rogues and Running*

Dogs where it is alleged: 'a four and a half month old Bedlington puppy' attacked a baited badger leaving some of its milk teeth in the brock. Bedlingtons still work badgers in some countries and the reports confirm they are still game unto death and indeed frequently they do die. For the British sportsman leave the badger well alone and avoid their well-known setts like the plague. Having said that I know of one active badger sett that is actually at the side of the road, so close in fact the badgers constantly dig out soil all over the road. Dog walkers constantly walk past it so how can they possibly avoid it? I am sure you will agree there is avoidance and avoidance, but where possible avoid all contact with badgers and their setts.

Badgers undoubtedly cause massive damage and even death to terriers and Bedlingtons as gutsy as they are often fell foul of the adder-like strike of the black and white. Continental terrier men in countries where it is still legal use Bedlingtons to badgers and these dogs still take tremendous punishment and give it too. The continent also offers tremendously courageous quarry in this animal whose savagery and fighting ability is second to none. It does not have an underground lair, it has no claws and its kidneys are not placed level like those of a true carnivore though meat is certainly not discarded in its diet, nothing is!

Another adversary is the wild swine or boar. A friend of mine in Slovakia works his Bedlingtons on wild boar and says the Bedlingtons attack the back of the boar. These game dogs do take them, but make no mistake he and his colleagues lose terriers to the wild swine; pigs, all pigs whether true wild boar, razor backs or feral pigs in Australia and New Zealand, are extremely savage and ferocious fighters. Terriers in packs can stop pigs but body armour and throat protection are a great advantage – the Australians use these on their dogs all the time.

Hunting the otter like the badger is strictly forbidden in the UK, whilst mink, stoat, weasel, grey squirrel and house mouse all fall foul of the current hunting with dogs laws in Britain and thus can only be hunted under exempted hunting. I will discuss this in the chapter on the law.

With permission and in season, dogs of all breeds, not just terriers, can take feathered game, which means pheasants, partridges, wildfowl (ducks and geese), woodcock, woodpigeons and corvids with the

Foxing Bedlington.

exception of the chough. Bedlington terriers and Bedlington lurchers (for some curious reason the Bedlington × whippet lurcher is very popular here) are on occasions very adept at taking both pheasants and partridges. My liver-coloured Bedlington lurcher Leo was a fantastic taker of feathered game, and in fact his first catch was a French red-legged partridge plucked from out of the air as it got airborne. Little Ninja, my last blue Bedlington stud dog, caught several pheasants in season when they foolishly ran instead of flew, though to be fair he crunched and killed his birds rather than giving a classic live gun dog retrieve, but retrieved they were albeit very dead and mangled.

The classic hunting/poaching/mooching Bedlington terrier was expected to secure feathered game and thankfully the working Bedlington can still legally do this today. All terriers and running dogs should be encouraged to catch feathered game unless you work your dogs on a game estate or shoot. I don't, though I do have quite a bit of permission where I can take and shoot pheasant, partridge and woodcock. So for the kitchen hunter the Bedlington and Bedlington lurcher can be quite a prize asset.

The Bedlington terrier in the past has been abused and used in highly atrocious and illegal activities, and it is sad but true that this has included both badger baiting and dog fighting. Allegedly crosses using Bedlington blood with the Staffordshire bull terrier and Kerry blue terrier have been used for this purpose. Both dog fighting and badger baiting are deplorable and those that partake in them can only expect to get what they deserve when they get caught.

Both the Bedlington terrier and the Bedlington lurcher are versatile dogs, highly adaptable working dogs that are adept at a multitude of tasks. One of the most memorable feats of working Bedlington prowess was seeing The Mad Ratter swim out to a clipped Canada goose, getting it and retrieving it back to hand to me, when the day was sub zero and Christmas dinner rested on his success!

Rock Star, a small blue bitch bred by Bill Brown in Manchester, not only spawned a dynasty but worked the spectrum and once caught a woodcock in season, whilst her great-granddaughter Lively Lucy, a beautiful sandy bitch, was proficient at taking mallard in the rushes. This bitch worked marvellously with Harris hawks, flushing mallard, pheasant and partridge for the raptor. Both Bedlingtons and Bedlington lurchers will work with birds of prey and of course ferrets. It is a nice team of workers when terrier, bird and ferret work together, and I have spent many happy winter days on gorse-laden hills returning home with a brace of rabbits, a pheasant and maybe a partridge, had some tea and then gone for a rabbit bash with 4×4 and rifle or lurcher. Working our dogs is really what it is all about.

The Bedlington terrier is very adaptable, and of course – the old argument, it will not go away – working type or outcrossed dogs will outperform the typical modern show stock. That adaptability can be seen perfectly when they are used in conjunction with raptors and ferrets. I actually do rate the Bedlington for hawk work and when used in unison with Harris or red tail buzzard, and occasionally goshawk, the results can be remarkable.

My son flies a large female Harris, a bird who has nailed several hares in her long and illustrious career that includes work to rats and rabbits on the lamp as well as the more traditional daytime work with ferrets, game birds and ducks. One autumn day the Harris hawk had 'tree'd' and in silent stoop had taken a large doe hare in her seat. The

Bedlington, a blue bitch out of John Piggin's Floyd of Eakring, had clearly picked up the hare's line and was working the field with obvious enthusiasm, quartering the ground like a spaniel. The Harris nailed her victim and then rode the bucking hare as it dragged the out-stretched-legged raptor along the ground, but in a trice our Bedlington was there thereby stopping a potentially dangerous war of attrition between predator and prey and also getting our beautiful jugged hare! Not once did that dog ever display aggression or jealousy to her co-hunter and that is how it should be. George Newcombe once said to me that he liked a dog with good common sense, and by and large Bedlingtons are just that.

My son and I have worked several Bedlingtons, both dogs and bitches, with Harris hawks, and their excellent nose and flushing ability has resulted in countless flights for the hawk and many good dinners for us, including teal, wigeon, rabbit, hare, partridge, pheasant and once a woodcock that hit a fence and could not get through. God bless the union of Harris hawk and Bedlington – an awesome team!

To all intents and purposes the only hunting in Britain unchanged is the pursuit of the rat and rabbit, others falling into the category 'exempted hunting' which varies from species to species and above and below ground. The mink is one such species that has presented lively hunting for hounds and terriers alike. The Bedlington has always been linked one way or another with otterhound-type dogs whether pocket-sized rough almost griffon type bassets or full-sized otterhounds, the so-called mink hound. As a pest species the mink is now widespread in the UK and it's getting more and more common. Not only is it a savage alien species but it is a threat to several British species, notably the water vole, various duck as well as moorhen and coots. When these species start to disappear on a fishery the water bailiffs should take note as mink will surely be present. With a liking for fish all in all the mink spells big trouble.

Bedlingtons just like Sealyham terriers love the water, and these two breeds also share their enthusiasm for hunting feral mink. My liver bitch Lively Lucy, a granddaughter of John Piggin's celebrated Floyd of Eakring, hunted mink with relish, killing several dozen during three memorable years at a local fishery. Some of these mink would hole up in ridiculous places like between the wooden pallets that made up some of the anglers' pegs around the lake, but one way or another we always managed to poke, entice or bolt out the mustelids.

Some mink have an almost nonchalant attitude about them displaying an arrogant lack of fear of man, but this rapidly changed when a dog or pack was on its pre-ban tail. Fearsome biters mink may well be but they are no match for most working terriers, lurchers or hounds. They are good swimmers and climbers of trees too but no match for fleet dogs if one is caught out on dry land. Hounds working with terriers accounted for numerous mink, so I find it ludicrous to think that any pest, not just the mink, has been afforded some protection under the hunting with dogs ban in the UK. However, the law is the law and until the day that the current legislation is changed we must obey the law of the land.

There is a story that concerns a pack of mink hounds hunting up a river pre ban on a large dog mink. After losing the mink, and casting around and not finding it the hounds drew on further up river to recommence hunting. Left behind were two terrier men with a solitary blue/black Bedlington bitch who had marked very strongly at a half-submerged small hole in the bank, but one follower had remarked that no mink was there and he bade farewell to the pair to hunt further upstream. The terrier men opened up the hole and with Bedlington barking, growling and digging on eventually brought the errant dog mink to book. As we all know Bedlingtons have great olfactory sense and this bitch was no exception.

From exempted hunting today back to the pre-ban days, fox, mink, otter, badger, rats and rabbits have all been the quarry of the terrier. Feathered game and wildfowl, both caught outright and brought down by the shooter, and days on the decoy fields after woodpigeon have been the province of the Bedlington terrier and the closely related lurcher.

9 The Law

In Britain we are subject to the Hunting Act 2004 which means in a nutshell it is illegal to hunt and kill any wild mammal with a dog, and that includes a mouse. What it does not include is the rat and rabbit, so both these species of mammals can still be hunted with dogs with no restrictions at all, and that is why packs of hounds can still hunt rabbits completely unhindered. However a person or persons can still hunt a fox underground provided certain conditions are met, and where these conditions are met it is called exempted hunting. Basically exempted hunting takes on two forms, above and below ground with one terrier below ground or two terriers in the case of the above-ground version. The purpose behind this is to flush out wild mammals to preserve wild birds and game birds.

To begin at the beginning, ALL hunting can only take place with the permission of the landowner or occupier, and this permission should be in writing. Rabbit control is all legal, whether it is flushing rabbits from cover or with the use of ferrets in daytime or by night, with the aid of a spot lamp or the use of long and occasionally gate nets. Ratting with terriers or running dogs (all dogs in fact) is also legal provided that a person has that said permission in writing. You can hunt rats both by day and night with dogs, but not the house mouse, so beware! The Hunting Act only applies to mammals, so provided a hunter has written permission a terrier or running dog owner can take in the relevant season's partridge, pheasant, duck or other feathered game. Pheasants have always been favourites amongst owners of working terriers and running dogs.

Once a pest has been flushed from below ground, for example a fox, it must be shot by a 'competent person' and this means in the case of the inevitable moving object a marksman with a shotgun. The bolting fox's escape route cannot be impeded by anything other than a net being placed over a hole. All this pest control is undertaken to protect wild and game birds.

Frances Fuller's Jasper Blue Drummer in Plashett stands alert for rabbits.

Other conditions to be met by the working terrier owner include the terrier being used to only flush the quarry and not fight with it, so only a 'soft' terrier is to be used below ground. Any terrier underground must be there for as short a time as possible and that terrier should be fitted with a locator collar (something that has already been voluntarily done for years!). Steps must be taken to minimise risk to all involved including the terrier and quarry. If a terrier is trapped underground prompt action needs to be taken to rescue and excavate the said terrier. (But, haven't working terrier enthusiasts always done this – it is called a dig!)

The hunting of foxes, mink, stoats, weasels, grey squirrels and mice is illegal unless certain conditions are met. These conditions are of course obtaining the obligatory written permission, and ensuring only

Slovakian hunters with Bedlingtons and fell terriers after a successful dig.

up to two terriers are used for above-ground flushing of wild mammals to the guns (or solitary gun). Above ground means cover such as woodland and undergrowth. I must say it conjures a somewhat odd vision of flushing a house mouse with two dogs and shooting that mouse with a shotgun! The above advice applies to all dog breeds. And that is the basic rule of thumb regarding working terriers under the Hunting Act in the UK.

Now to the law regarding running dogs: this means lurchers, all sight hounds (whippets, greyhounds, deerhounds, salukis, etc.). It is legal to take rabbits by day or night, and these can be coursed or caught in conjunction with ferrets; the same applies to rats. Again this should have the appropriate written permission. What you cannot do is course hares either brown or blue, for coursing is illegal, and it is also illegal in fact to organise or attend any type of hare-coursing event. But, hares may still be shot after being flushed by two dogs. There is always the possibility of a hare inadvertently being flushed by a running dog such as a lurcher and the dog 'accidentally' chasing it. When and if this happens you the owner/handler of the dog MUST take immediate action to stop that pursuit. The police have a very wide range of powers of confiscation if they suspect you have been up to an illegal activity with hunting dogs and they are empowered to confiscate dogs, equipment and vehicles.

Driven shooting and using dogs seems to be fairly safe ground, for here the intention is very clearly not the taking of a wild mammal but rather game birds, and we already have established both terriers and lurchers can legally take pheasants, partridges, etc. within their respective shooting seasons, as long as the landowner agrees to this and grants the hunter written permission.

Rough shooting can present something more of a problem in that it can be difficult to prove that no one was actually intending to hunt a wild mammal. Problems can arise and very often these situations come about when some well-intentioned member of the non-field sports community ends up calling the police or RSPCA when they suspect a 'crime' has been committed. Long before the Hunting Act was ever implemented general members of Joe Public often reported alleged atrocities, and these usually involved badger digging which had been confused with badger baiting. In many cases these incidents involved innocent lampers or ferret enthusiasts. Twice I can think of officers being called to the countryside to investigate alleged misdemeanours and on both occasions they were innocent. I know, I was there!

The first was an incident involving lamping when a friend and I noticed a police car near our van just after commencing legal lamping. A local had noticed the van and light and, working on the premise that badgers frequented the area, reported alleged badger baiting. Clearly this was rubbish and no action was taken, other than proving our legal right to be there.

The other occasion involved a police officer trudging across a field to investigate another alleged badger crime. The officer arrived just as I broke through a tube to extract a rabbit that my ferret had blocked up in a stop end in a very active rabbit warren. Again another well-meaning member of the local community had 'reported' it to the local constabulary and again it was proven we were innocent. Be aware that activities with both terriers and running dogs in the countryside do attract unwelcome if not sometimes well-meaning attention.

For rough shooting a dog may be used when flushing for a hare or fox but now it is classed as hunting and is covered by the Hunting Act. And it is important to remember the following when using dogs to flush wild mammals. This is permissible when carried out to reduce damage to crops, wild and game birds, to protect livestock food, growing timber and fisheries. Also, as before full written permission is required, no dog is to be used underground and no more than two dogs are to be used. Wild mammals need to be shot dead by a 'competent person'; this is I assume a person with considerable experience with a shotgun and the said person must hold the relevant certificate and of course is using a licensed weapon. Do follow the letter of the law when working dogs, whether terriers, running dogs or flushing to guns.

My express thanks go to the Countryside Alliance for their kind help in giving advice on this complex Act.

10 Working Shows and Internet Forums

Working terrier and lurcher shows are extremely popular events, of this there can be no denying. During the spring, summer and early autumn months absolutely loads of these events take place the length and breadth of Britain, and more and more of these shows cater for the Bedlington terrier. Is that a good thing? Taken to its logical conclusion and on face value you have to say yes, but if we delve a little deeper however one can see it is fraught with certain problems which can in some cases (though not all I should stress) make it something of a mockery, a purely farcical event.

I have in the past supported these shows especially when Bedlington classes have been scheduled alongside the usual Jack Russell, Lakeland/fell and Border terrier classes. I remember going to one such show back in the day and entering three terriers in a three class entry (so of course all were mine). The hapless judge confessed to me he hadn't realised there were Bedlington classes scheduled for that day and that he hadn't got a clue what he was looking for. Well at least ten out of ten for his honesty! To conclude this debacle he still got his decision totally wrong and picked the worst best and the best third – I think I was unbiased as I owned all three! Like most people I supported these events believing it was good publicity for the Bedlington terrier, but it seems I may have been wrong.

Not all working terrier shows are of this ilk though, and happily the best examples of these are those I have had the privilege of being involved with to some degree. I was Chairman of the Working Type Bedlington Terrier Association, which worked closely with the Heart of England Lurcher Society in its show events. The WTBTA had a strong policy of only using select working judges at its events and also would supply or recommend judges for any interested parties who were thinking of staging working Bedlington classes at their events. This was a good idea then and is still a great idea now.

The thing is the WTBTA no longer exists which is a great pity for this very simple concept worked superbly. John Piggin, Nigel Evans and I judged at WTBTA or at Heart of England Lurcher Society events – working Bedlington judges judging working Bedlingtons. Perfect! Years went by and I was then asked to judge a show just outside Leeds. The event had the usual lurcher and terrier classes but it scheduled a full sporting Lucas terrier and working Bedlington terrier programme; in fact it was advertised as a sporting Lucas and Bedlington show. The show was very well promoted and D.B. Plummer was also in attendance at the event. The scene was set for a great day, but what I didn't envisage was the number of Bedlingtons there that day – the entrants numbered nearly a hundred! Incredible for a working terrier show.

The following year I was asked once again to judge it but I declined wanting someone else to do the honours. John Holden of Granitor Bedlingtons judged the entrants, and I gather the numbers were even slightly greater, which was really fantastic for a working terrier show.

Since that time working terrier shows have staged classes for working Bedlingtons, and usually it is the non-specialist working terrier judge who views the dogs. This is OK to a degree but not all the time, given that some judges view a dog purely as an earth dog, and what works for a Lakeland does not necessarily work for a Bedlington terrier. Do you pick a large but typical Bedlington terrier over a poor small

Gutchcommon-bred Bedlingtons bred by the author.

dog? Of course you do, but sadly that doesn't always happen, for I have seen some horrendous decisions made by respected working terrier judges, and furthermore how often does the BOB Bedlington go on to take best in show terrier? Not very often, I can tell you. The old suggestion that working classes for Bedlingtons at shows are good publicity for working Bedlingtons is therefore a difficult one to substantiate, but nonetheless if the judge is one who is familiar and has worked Bedlingtons the whole venture could be a worthwhile one.

Jamie, owned by Margaret Williamson.

So, how do we make a working terrier show that includes Bedlington classes creditable? Already we have some country fairs that do carry some respect from the working Bedlingtons' angle. The Heart of Wales Game Fair and The Welsh Game Fair are two from Wales obviously, and both are well attended by Bedlington fans. Judges do need to have experience working Bedlingtons.

When I judge Bedlington terriers I don't always span them, though on obvious ones I sometimes do, especially if it is a dog with some substance rather than a small weedy specimen (which are always spannable). I am drawing attention to this dog, perhaps to the onlookers, and nearly always if this dog has a good coat and is balanced it will be in the prize winners. I will never attempt to span a large specimen, for clearly this type of dog was never in the history of the breed designed to go to ground. A large animal at any time in the breed's history clearly had other legitimate uses. There have always been large and small Bedlingtons of the correct type; variance in size occurs within the same litter so it therefore follows we should not decry the outsize Bedlington. A working Bedlington judge should know this in any case. The general rule of thumb is that Bedlington owners should be Bedlington judges, and on some occasions (though not all) the judge of conventional working terriers may well find himself out on a limb.

Personally I like to see balanced, long-backed terriers, dogs with strong jaws and teeth but a head not out of proportion with the rest of the dog. Flat ribs with a rise over the loins, a long hare foot and a coat of a double hard linty texture. The terrier needs to be dark but not black or chocolate, and it needs an almost white silky top knot; insufficient leg furnishings should not penalise the terrier for it is irrelevant in a working-type Bedlington, and that last description is vital – WORKING TYPE! Show dogs whether workers or not, or indeed pets, fail here. My goal is to see Bedlingtons we could call justifiably 'work and show', just as it used to be.

It is the fault of show judges picking untypical dogs. It needs not just an isolated judge to pick one winner of the right type, but there needs to be a complete shift. A pure-bred Bedlington of working type, a dog just as KC registered as any show dog, is a joy to behold, it is essential to the future well-being of all Bedlingtons, and it's the type of dog that would be sought by owners of outcrossed dogs (maybe linty coated terriers?). Working Bedlington classes should never be farcical, always positive and never ever a mockery.

I believe special classes should be drawn up for hybrid dogs as I really do believe there is a place for the black dog, but not as a Bedlington rather more as a linty coated terrier. The latter becoming a separate entity would be the greatest accolade breeders of such terriers could have bestowed upon them. To conclude, working Bedlington classes or shows are a really nice idea; what isn't however is the event that degenerates into a farce simply because the judge has not got experience with the WORKING-TYPE BEDLINGTON TERRIER.

Working shows for Bedlingtons have been deemed in the past good publicity for the breed. This is something everyone hoped for but after showing some optimism in this direction, Margaret Williamson and George Newcombe both voiced doubts as to the validity of such events. Firstly in the 1980s when working Bedlington classes were included at some terrier and lurcher shows certain 'rosette' hunters were bringing along anything, even dogs in show trim, and these were winning. Owners of other working terriers, the Jack Russells, Lakeland/fells and Borders of this world, clearly saw these terriers as the imposters that they were, and it all had a counterproductive feel about it.

Nonetheless some organisations such as the Fell and Moorland

Working Terrier Club did make an attempt to promote the breed as a working terrier, and they did some homework and got judges who actually knew one end of a Bedlington from another, whilst certain other shows in the north of England did put on good attempts at catering correctly for the Bedlington. Generally however the average hunt show with just two classes for the breed often as not failed. Few judges knew what to look for, for they were thrown in at the deep end and went one way or the other, ending up picking a show dog or some- times untypical undocked mongrels that may or may not have had some passing resemblance to the Bedlington terrier.

Of late certain Welsh Country Fairs have fared much better with both Bedlington classes and attendances at these events, and the most notable of these are The Welsh Game Fair and The Heart of Wales Fair, the latter usually attracting a good number of dogs. Let us hope more and more informed judges are picked and greater interest in the Bedlington brings about a much brighter outcome for what essentially should be an interesting and fun event, but equally so an event that does promote the correct type of dog and not create a farce.

The internet has opened up all sorts of possibilities regarding working dogs and field sports in general. Indeed with the lack of any kind of working organisation or club for working Bedlingtons, the internet with its various websites and forums has provided a real alternative to the now absent 'working' clubs. Several internet forums have sections that from time to time carry threads regarding working Bedlingtons, whilst some running dog forums include a section for terriers or 'anything else'. I now provide a selection of internet forums and websites that owners of working Bedlingtons may find of interest.

The Hunting Life often carries features and threads that members can contribute to when they join. Their terrier section is extensive. The Working Whippet Forum is a site I personally like but that is also due to the fact that I keep and work a pure whippet (another breed I care about tremendously). This internet site often carries threads on Bedlingtons. Jeff Hutchings, one of the site's administrators, is also a great admirer of Bedlingtons who keeps a Bedlington and sometimes breeds a litter of genuine Bedlington × whippet pups. As a footnote to this readers may be interested to visit the websites of Pennymeadow Whippets and Beddywhippets.

Probably the most obvious choice for the owner of the working Bedlington will be the Working Bedlington Forum, a site that has been in existence since 2007. It is a sometimes colourful forum that often gets a little heated, nonetheless it does cover some great topics and debates. It is an internet site that everyone who keeps Bedlingtons and has access to the web should check out. This site is possibly the nearest we will get to a working Bedlington organisation and I feel it should be supported, for an organisation like this may well make a much better lot for the Bedlington at working shows or country fairs. Indeed the Working Bedlington Forum is gathering momentum and respect at a tremendous rate, its site administrators do a tremendous job and the cause of the real Bedlington terrier can only benefit from its existence.

Another site I personally like and sometimes visit for its general terrier and running dog content (though not generally Bedlington it must be stressed) is not one based in the UK. It is Ozziedoggers, and as its name suggests it is an Australian forum site. The subjects covered are as on those previously mentioned UK sites, very varied and sometimes heated but always good entertainment and often a good source of information. It is nice to see the different attitudes they have abroad (and the different laws) to ours in Britain, plus get an insight into their varied quarry.

All forums seem to have members from abroad, often including Bedlington owners from other countries, which again makes for a much greater perspective when we look at the great potential of the Bedlington. I think that we can all benefit from all the internet forums and websites that are available to us, after all they are so easy to access and the information is so quick. A word of caution, however, the debates on most forums can often get heated and sometimes quite personal. Site administrators usually are quite strict and calmly keep things as civil as they should be, but if you are of a sensitive nature you may find some things a little disturbing.

They can do a lot of good for field sports, but potentially they can do harm too. The way it works is simplicity in itself. We have a collection of laws in the UK and like them or not we have to adhere them rigidly, for to do otherwise is not only illegal, but would bring the legitimate sports into disrepute and also give vital political ammunition to those who seek to see our legal activities curtailed, and that basically means the eventual banning of field sports in general or as our opponents term them, blood sports, including angling.

Like it or not hare coursing is banned. The hunting of the fox as we once knew it is also forbidden, except for exempted hunting (see the chapter on the law). It works the same with other species too, whilst others like the badger and otter were outlawed long before the current laws came into place (again see my chapter on the law). When pictures are published on sites or forums with deer or some- times hares that clearly have been taken illegally, or indeed threads using 'code talk' such as 'long ears', 'large rabbits' (hares) or 'barkers' (muntjac deer) no one is being fooled except perhaps the authors of such threads. The anti-field sports factions trawl the internet and would find it immensely easy to gain access to the sites. For goodness sake it's bad enough having to contend with the antis' objection to legitimate field sports without giving them vital information that will eventually one day sound the death knell on all field sports as we know them in Britain. I urge all site owners to be vigilant and also conversant with the current laws in the UK, because for our sports to continue we need to be squeaky clean and that means site administrators being vigilant and keeping threads within the law regarding field sports. Reference to forbidden quarry can be discussed in a historical context, and that is why this book makes frequent reference to 'pre ban'. That is just the way it is. Even I have had experience with antis regarding a video we published on You Tube on the internet, and that was just a ferreting clip. So beware, the antis do trawl the field sports sites.

Readers may be interested to enter into a search engine 'John Glover's Country Pursuits', as my website carries lots of my articles, many from the past but also exclusives to the website. Naturally there is a lot of working Bedlington-orientated articles and also a lot about working dogs, ferrets and general field sports too. I hope you enjoy your visit and maybe make yourself a member.

Internet forums are great as long as the site administrators do their job well, and the Working Whippet Forum is the one all working dog forums should aspire to, for it is well run, friendly and makes for informative entertainment. I hope all forums follow their example.

Rules are there for the good of all concerned but on some occasions they are there for the muscle of the site administrators. The Working Whippet Forum with its varied topics and well-run ideals is the one most should aspire too.

11 Long Live the Bedlington

We have come to a period in the book when we must look at the future of the working, sporting, hunting Bedlington terrier. Before this however we need to look at some of the qualities or otherwise that have forged our breed. Since 1782 we have been able to trace back the ancestors of the Bedlington terrier to Old Flint, and in fact modern show dogs can even be traced back to this dog. This makes that pedigree unique as it is the oldest pedigree in existence.

We can be certain terriers of the day never went under a name: not Rothbury, not Northumberland fox terrier, and certainly not Bedlington. In those far-off days they were called just terriers. All that mattered was that the dogs worked, and that they worked and worked well was never in doubt. Neither is there doubt that these terriers were dual purpose, not only capable of thrashing a fox to death if it refused to bolt but also having speed and gameness enough to tackle and sometimes kill quarry above ground. It is the original lurcher-like terrier that the wild boar hunters of Eastern Europe find endearing in their working Bedlingtons in modern times.

The collective terriers of the border regions of England and Scotland may have at one time been variable in type but what they would all have in common is undoubted gameness, for early Dandie Dinmonts, Borders and prototype Bedlingtons (Rothburys) were exceedingly hard and brave dogs. They had to be. Border land foxes often holed up in rock lairs that were not only difficult to dig but downright dangerous, and to have a dog that would close and kill its fox was a great advantage.

Badgers had always been a traditional quarry of the Border land terriers and William Allen could confidently sell the skin of any otter once his dogs (Peachem and Pincher) 'gave mouth on the trail of an otter'. The Allens were said to be of the Yetholm tribe of Gypsy stock, a family who lived around the Rothbury area catching animals that could be either used in the pot or sold for that purpose. A small hound-type of terrier was beginning to evolve with a unique voice and baying tongue, a terrier that would pack together but not suffer fools, a dog with common sense and a good level of obedience that regarded everything from mouse to badger as its foe. Rabbits were never sniffed at, the working class poor or the resilient Gypsies regarding the humble rabbit as a virtual life saver when times were hard and it was the only potential protein source. Hares too were taken in their seats, squealing into the icy dawns or run down by, for example, a basset or beagle.

What set the Bedlington apart from both the Dandie Dinmont and Border terrier was the breed's tendency to produce both large and small puppies within the same litter. This still happens today: Floyd of Eakring's sire Kentenes Rogue was a tiny scrap of a Gutchcommon-bred dog whilst Floyd was a large, albeit nice type of sandy-coloured Bedlington. It is my firm belief some type of black and tan, or blue and tan rough-coated scent hound entered into the Bedlington's early make up. This dog would certainly have been a type of otterhound, though maybe a little smaller than today's counterpart, possibly shorter in the leg making it reminiscent of a griffon basset type. After all, these little hounds in modern times are fantastic hunting dogs. Nick Valentine runs this type of dog in a rabbit pack, and I have hunted with them, catching over twenty rabbits in the day. Believe me, it was wonderful sport in the beautiful Devon countryside. It is my belief that you could breed a useful hybrid worker from a Bedlington and one of these small, very useful rough-coated hounds. Question is, has something similar to this happened before? I certainly believe it could have done.

Joseph Ainsley, who lived from 1800–1871, is generally credited as the founder of the breed by changing the terrier's name from Rothbury to Bedlington. However, in 1998 Curran Cooper in her privately published *Warts and All, A Pictorial History of the Bedlington Terrier* goes to some length to discredit some of the so-called facts. The picture on page three of good old Joe is one of the discrepancies Curran Cooper allegedly identifies. The picture is usually credited as Ainsley with Young Piper and Phoebe. Curran Cooper believed that the terriers in the pictures were not these dogs, and furthermore the name Ainsley should be Aynsley. However, Ken Bounden in his book *The Bedlington Terrier*, uses the spelling Ainsley, as do the majority of people. The terriers in the picture have always had a look of Border about them, as odd as it may seem. I have to say the dogs have never impressed me, that's for sure, and neither does the picture of William Clark (1817–1881) with the very coarse-looking Scamp, and in my opinion its ugly dam, Daisy.

By the time T.J. Pickett's Tyneside had been whelped in 1869 the Bedlington had developed into a beautiful balanced breed as George Earl's painting of the bitch revealed. Another famous early Bedlington was Newcastle Lad (1872) that at one stage belonged to Suffolk enthusiast John Cornforth, who was also the owner of the allegedly 'weak legged' Nelson. But Nelson arrived on the scene ten years later.

A famous Bedlington with a superb long flexible back was Ch. Miss Oliver, a liver bitch bred by one Mr Pratt. Her owner became largely well known for his Cranley Bedlingtons due to Ch. Miss Oliver's success in the show ring. The Bedlington terrier had come of age; it had started out as a purely working terrier and was now elevated to the status of show dog.

The dogs of the late nineteenth century were of a different ilk to many of today's show bench champions, especially those exhibited in Scandinavia and the USA. In 1899 Mrs Smith's Breakwater dogs certainly were beautifully long-backed dogs – show dogs but animals any working terrier enthusiast would be proud to own. The Bedlington terrier of the time justified its status of work and show, for its reputation as a hard-bitten destroyer of subterranean vermin was well known and its liking for aquatic environments not only made it a favourite to take otter when it was legal and of course rats, but substantiated the suggestion of some link to a scent hound ancestor, possibly a type of otterhound.

Another noteworthy consideration is the dark-coloured brindled terrier of the Ullswater area. The so-called Ullswater terrier had been bred by the Earls of Lonsdale at Lowther Castle since 1732. Were these the forerunners of the fell terriers that would be termed the true Patterdale terrier? Not only were brindles found but also blues and very light tan. How much of this fell-type breeding was found around the Border areas in the late eighteenth century and did any of it find

149

Sarah Whetstone with Chris Mulreidy's outcrossed dogs enjoying a day ferreting.

its way into the Bedlington gene pool? We know the real Patterdale terrier (not the black and red fell types) was influenced by the Bedlington, but could it be that this fell breeding played a part in the history leading to these fell types being referred to as just 'terriers' just as the early Rothbury types were? Where the brindle element comes from in these so-called Bedlingtons is anybody's guess. Some say it came from the fighting dog influence of the Black Country foundry workers who came to stay in the Rothbury area in the 1800s. Or might it have been from a much closer source geographically to the Bedlington than where the foundry workers' dogs came from?

The ancestry of Tommy Dobson's fell terriers was much more well known, as is fact it was he who saw the viability of breeding in Bedlington blood to his line of fell terriers. Dobson's fell × Bedlington hybrids were being bred and worked around the turn of the twentieth century. Brian Plummer writing in *Shooting Times & Country Magazine* in February 1982 makes mention of Dobson using 'a strain of chocolate Bedlington bred round Egremont in the 1800s'. Being described as 'chocolate' speaks volumes of the colour intensities of the Bedlington's coat. I recently had a picture sent to me of a chocolate and tan Bedlington × Lakland hybrid, and it was exactly the same type as those hybrids that Tommy Dobson had in the early 1900s.

By the time of the Salters Hall Wood Badger dig of 1917 the working qualities of the

Margaret Williamson, the judge at Darlington – date unknown.

151

Bedlington terrier were well known, even if some terriers paid the ultimate price while engaging brock underground. Badger-digging clubs or parties were springing up all over England during the run up to the hostilities of the Great War, and there was an air of respectability about the taking of brock with terriers. Very often badgers were dug to, tongued and sacked up. They didn't go to the pits to be baited by bull-blooded fighting dogs but instead they were liberated back to freedom. It would of course be highly illegal for anyone to do this nowadays on two counts: it's illegal to dig a badger and it's illegal to release any captured animal anywhere else, be it rabbit, rat or fox.

By the time the hostilities of both World Wars had ended, the terrier had survived and showing once again came to the fore. The Bedlington world had witnessed the emergence of the Misses Maunsell and Hamilton, Mrs M.K.M. Williamson had registered the prefix Worton and then changed it to Gutchcommon (named after a common in Semley, which it is said attracted various travellers who had with them surly poaching dogs, possibly Bedlingtons but definitely lurchers) and one George Newcombe had bought his first Bedlington and started showing. It wasn't long before Newcombe had decided showing was not for him and his lifelong obsession with working his terriers began, and whilst his pure-bred Rillingtons didn't have quite the same history as the Gutchcommon strain or the quality of coat of that strain, they did have high prey drive and entered to fox easily.

Fred Gent's Foggyfurze lines had had some influence in George's dogs, and in fact Newcombe once told me early Foggyfurze stock was superb in type and nature. What little bit of Foggyfurze breeding I had in my stock George quite openly told me he preferred to my Gutch-common-saturated breeding. It is true I didn't see eye to eye with George on many things towards the end of our relationship, as in little things like the taking of foxes with lurchers, pre ban of course, where George felt it was the right of the fox-hunting packs and not the right of the working lurcher keeper. He didn't agree with me on Gutchcom-mon breeding either, though that didn't stop him using Gutchcommon George as an outcross.

All in all George Newcombe was a great working Bedlington terrier man. He will never be forgotten and when he died he left a gaping hole in the world of the working Bedlington. He was by nature controversial, a passionate hunter and dedicated countryman; I still remember sitting in his house in Rillington, North Yorkshire and him plucking a bumble-bee from his living room window, and quite calmly and without fear of being stung liberating the angry buzzing insect out of the opened window. I would just like to acknowledge the memories I have personally of George Newcombe and thank him for all the help he gave me.

I remember George saying to me once about how he could visualise the Dandie Dinmont terrier, way back in time working the banks of the River Coquet whilst hunting otter and working to both fox and badger on the lower reaches of the Coquet Valley. There are few Dandies worked nowadays and certainly none of any working strain. One very, very rarely sees advertisements for working Dandies, and in over twenty years I can only once think of one with a Dandie Dinmont connection and that was in a lurcher advertisement in *The Country-man's Weekly*. Yes, working Dandies are certainly thin on the ground!

The Bedlington terrier's biggest fault lies its small gene pool. From its conception as a type to its establishment as a breed, the genetic potential has been small. Inbreeding as we know went on in the very earliest days of the breed. By the time the Second World War had ended and once again show champions began to emerge, certain stud dogs were being used over and over again, and yet more inbreeding took place.

The possible introduction of poodle blood has always been a controversial point and one on which George Newcombe did have very strong views. Newcombe was convinced of poodle breeding in modern show dogs, and so are a host of others including me, although it has been one the show world has denied vehemently. In fact it has been branded about since the times of Redmarshall in his *The Bedlington Terrier – History and Origin* for he wrote and I quote: 'I am satisfied in my own mind that it did, as I have seen dogs whose owners stated they were Bedlington cross poodles.'

Newcombe also related to me how he saw outcrossing, stating how to a degree characteristics can be saved within a pure breed but only if they are there in the first place. Early Rillington stock certainly had a fiery and aggressive outlook towards British vermin, being feisty and keen to avenge any insult (as I have said, the only ferret I have ever had killed was by a Rillington-bred bitch and that was George's Donna), but they were handy dogs to use.

With the advent of George's outcrossed stock the pure-bred Rillingtons dwindled whilst it is true the hybrid stock increased and this is what Newcombe sold latterly. I doubt, in fact I am fairly certain that no such thing as a pure-bred Rillington exists nowadays. Gutchcommon stock were much more common as there were well-known Gutchcommon stud dogs siring pups after Margaret Williamson's era. These included Roy Mee's Rogue of Birkacre and Kentenes Rogue (litter brothers), John Piggin's Jasper of Kentene and my own The Mad Ratter and his son Rat Pit Billy; from these five dogs numerous Gutchcommon and Gutchcommon-saturated dogs were bred. I am sure significantly more Gutchcommon were bred over the years than Rillington strain dogs.

As more and more Gutchcommon dogs were bred so began a trend to introduce them into show stock; sometimes this was intentional, other times not so. Roy Mee of Leicester tried (unsuccessfully I might add) to get the controversial Roddy registered with the Kennel Club, but the fact that a stud fee hadn't been paid to John Piggin meant that however good Roddy was he would never be registered. I had Roddy, and found him to be an aggressive kind of mixed-up dog, which was understandable when one realises how many homes he had known. In the end he couldn't be worked near other dogs but his physical qualities were without doubt. Lois Sutton, a show enthusiast of some note, used him to one of her exhibition dogs and produced a wonderful litter, but eventually it was obvious Roddy would never be registered so with heavy heart Lois sold her unregistered pups to pet homes, for no matter how good they were they would never become show dogs. Nonetheless Lois could see how good Gutchcommon coats were, and she was not alone in this.

Coats have always been a bone of contention (for example, you would be amazed how many people think that white is a recognised colour in the Bedlington) and to be honest the Americans and Scandinavians have done little to diminish this by breeding utterly untypical dogs. Nevertheless, recently I have been impressed by breeders of Bedlingtons such as Frances Fuller and Lesley Caines who strive to breed good-coated dogs both in colour and texture. Obviously good coats are to be recommended in any working dog and especially so in a Bedlington when even a good-coated one fails to compare with a Lakeland terrier for example, despite the fact that the Lakeland owes so much of its genetic make up to the Bedlington terrier. George Newcombe, that champion of the working Bedlington, related a story to me where a lady whom he once knew had line bred Lakeland terriers for many years when out of the blue a perfect liver-coloured Bedlington terrier appeared in one of her litters.

Coats were one thing but size for work underground had always been a contentious subject amongst working Bedlington aficionados. In and amongst small types big types appeared from time to time. These large terriers were much prized amongst the lurcher breeding fraternity for they possessed everything their smaller brethren had with the exception of being able to go to ground with comparative ease. These larger hound types were perfectly natural and a legacy of a water dog of some type, possibly a otterhound.

The Bedlington fire is legendary. Indeed they will fight at the drop of a hat given the chance. No doubt this drew the attention of travelling stock who were not averse to a few hours of 'cocking' (cock fighting), fighting involving men fighting other men, pulping their faces into bloody red messes with their bare knuckles, but also dog versus dog contests. The capital of the country and the English Midlands had already embraced dog fighting where bull and terriers fought each other in deathly pit matches, and Scotland too had its share of dog fighters with their massive, almost mastiff types known as Blue Pauls, huge monsters often weighing up to 100 lbs. But despite their power their slowness meant this type of combat found little favour with the southern pit fighters.

Around Rothbury the travellers used their Bedlingtons for fighting, and often baited badgers with their game blue and liver dogs. We know that the breed needed plenty of pluck to close and kill reluctant Border land, fell, moor and Lakeland foxes, and this they had in abundance. The pit-fighting fancy also matched their dogs or rat-hunting tykes against rats in a pit not dissimilar to that of a dog pit. It was here, often in gas light, that terriers gave account of themselves on a Friday night. All manner of terriers participated in the carnage and Margaret Williamson of Gutchcommon fame remembers talk of them even in southern England.

Bull blood is allegedly in the make up of the Bedlington terrier. The introduction of bull-blood breeding has been tried and tested and still goes on today to produce working dogs as this ratter belonging to Yvonne Tilbury testifies.

Smooth fox terriers or Jack Russell types were invariably popular especially if the latter was on the leg. Staffordshire bull terrier-type dogs were said to be better on a hundred rats if not several hundred, but for the pitmen of Durham and the whole of the north-east of England there was only one dog – the Bedlington terrier. Speaking of northern pitmen did this mean colliers or pitmen who took part in baiting and fighting sports? It is open for debate that is for sure! These northern sporting dog fanciers certainly rated gameness and downright reckless hardness in their dogs. They too were hard men living in dire poverty and like their terriers entered the inky blackness of the earth's bowels often going to work 'down pit' before daybreak and returning if they were lucky in that self-same darkness. The weekends were a brief respite before Monday morning came round all too quickly. The oft-heard saying of 'hard times beget hard men' rings exceptionally true here. Despite this hardness and seemingly uncaring disposition there burned a sensitive side within these hard battle-scarred men for many of them were exceptional stock men capable of bringing out the best in either fighting or baiting dogs, rat pit tykes, rag-racing whippets, fighting cocks or racing pigeons and an entire rustic science quietly flowed within their very life blood.

There are still those who consider the Bedlington terrier to be the result of a Dandie Dinmont/whippet union, and whilst it may be true that some working terrier blood (possibly Bedlington terrier?) could have contributed to the make up of the working and racing whippet, there is absolutely no evidence to support the notion that it worked the other way, namely that the whippet had a place in the Bedlington terrier's creation. What they did have in common was blind, reckless dead gameness, and in fact there is evidence to suggest that black-masked light fawns in Staffordshire bull terriers were only found after whippets of this colouration were hybridised with Black Country pit dogs. Margaret Williamson recounts a story of once stopping in a town with her car and leaving some Bedlingtons in the vehicle, and when she got back she found an utterly overjoyed old boy enthusing over the 'good old days' when he used to catch live rats to 'test the Bedlingtons on a Friday night down the pub'. It seems Bedlingtons were particularly popular in the southern part of England as well as their traditional homeland of the English north-east.

All this had been going on while the show fancy had got stronger and more and more popular, but the knock-on effect was that true working Bedlington terriers were surviving amongst these working terrier men and pitmen. The alternative Bedlington terrier name of pitmans terrier came about because of this, but whether the 'pit' meant

My grandfather with a Sealyham-related breed through the Dandie Dinmont.

mine or dog or baiting pit is open for debate. Whatever the truth was does not matter one iota – the fox-hunting Bedlington of the fells was coming to the fore, and from then on certain working terrier men started to use Bedlington blood to fire up flagging strains and types of working terriers just as Tommy Dobson had done at the turn of the twentieth century. One World War later, fell men and Welsh colliers alike were using fiery Bedlington blood to introduce northern-coloured terriers and Welsh white-bodied dogs remarkably similar to a Sealyham type of working terrier.

Not much got past these terriers either. My own grandfather spoke of a Sealyham type of dog that was a result of a Bedlington crossed to a Sealyham-type Jack Russell that had been mated back to a Sealyham. This predominantly white-bodied dog let nothing past it in an earth even if it could not on some occasions get right up to its fox. This reminds me of several dogs in the past where, although they may have been a shade too large and somewhat coarse, were totally reliable as finders and stayers. This is an essential quality for once a fox is staying put in an earth a terrier needs to stick to its quarry and not let its fox past it in a tube. It is a prime quality.

Over the years there have always been quality large Bedlingtons, and these were the dogs reminiscent of the old catch dog of Rothbury, the terrier which nailed both fox and hare above ground. In more re-cent times there have been some exceptional large Bedlingtons, including Floyd belonging to John Piggin, and Blue belonging to George Newcombe, but one of the nicest was a mas-sive dog owned by Frances

Red, three-quarters Bedlington, one-quarter Glen of Imaal, sire Sam, dam Newcombe's Donna. Bred by author.

Fuller of Plashett Bedlingtons. It was a beast of a dog called Bruno, tech-nically a liver-coloured dog but in reality a chocolate-coloured dog, and the fact that he was nineteen inches to the shoulder is immaterial, as pictures show a powerfully built dog with a physique that suggests great stamina. If I nit-picked over him at all it would be because I would have liked to see a lighter top knot, but that's about all.

We have already established that Bedlingtons are good at packing together and the breed is well blessed in both nose and stamina, making for a great bobbery pack with Bedlingtons right at the heart of it. In bygone days when hare hunting was permissible it was always likely Bedlingtons would pick up a hare's line. We have mentioned this previously in the chapter on the quarry – the head down and the relentless beagle-like casting around until the quarry is relocated is a hallmark of the breed's olfactory sense (again I believe the legacy of a hound ancestor), and that tremendous stamina and unwavering pursuit were synonymous with hare hunters.

I believe these big dogs to have been favoured by the sportsmen and Gypsies of the late 1700s for they were true dual-purpose dogs providing both meat and saleable fox, otter and marten pelts. There is certainly something very evocative and reminiscent of hunting with hounds in a Bedlington bobbery pack, from the way they hunt to their music or baying when they find quarry. Today's rabbit hunters can confirm this, as indeed I can.

How have our working strains changed in recent years? The Gutch-common strain was very popular in the 1970s, '80s and '90s but a trend had drifted in that had diluted the true Gutchcommon dog. Sadly by the 1990s the strain had become very inbred in my opinion. In its heyday in the 1960s and '70s the Gutchcommon strain not only sold well but was being promoted as *the* real Bedlington terrier. I have never made any secret of the fact that I liked the strain, but nevertheless there were certain things about the type I would have changed. Roy Mee of Leicester really rated the strain and quite rightly so for as an ideally sized dog with a good working jacket on it the Gutchcommon Bedlington was just not going to be bettered. During the 1980s and '90s the strain was happily still being worked by some genuine pre-ban fox-hunting enthusiasts.

But not all! Others coming into the breed saw the strain or deriva-tives of it as purely a financial investment, a terrier they could cash in on and make some money, and, guess what, that happened. Pups were frequently sold under the misleading 'Gutchcommon-bred puppies for sale', when in actual fact they may have had very little of that breeding in them. A similar situation happened with Rillington Bedlingtons, and Newcombe took grave exception to people using his strain's name as an advertising medium; in fact I am certain George lost one or two friends along the way due to this very fact. Numerically Rillington Bedlingtons were significantly fewer than their Gutchcom-mon counterparts, but that didn't stop folk cashing in on both families of Bedlingtons.

Roy Mee had tirelessly bred his improved Gutchcommon dogs including true sandys as opposed to liver-coloured specimens, and they did need to be improved for latterly I thought the dogs showed a tendency to have a rather pointed bottom jaw and teeth that were becoming smaller. The coats were, however, still out of this world for a Bedlington – the blues were beautiful blue/black and the top knots almost white and silky to the touch. Jack Walker of Shepshed in Leicestershire had a wonderful bitch of the type just described bought I believe from Roy Mee; this dog had ample opportunity to work and did, her only physical fault being an undershot jaw. Nevertheless, I gave her Best Bedlington at a Heart of England Lurcher Society show held at The Furnace Inn in Bedworth one bitterly cold, snowy November day.

The livers from the Gutchcommon strain were probably better than the blues in my opinion, though to be fair I have always favoured the browns over the blues, one example being my own The Mad Ratter. He was another pre-ban foxing dog whose

Granitor dogs.

name was sometimes capitalised upon and exploited, but I suppose it could have been mute testimony to a Bedlington who forged a reputation for never taking a backward step in his working career. There was certainly a greater range of colours in the Gutchcommon Bedlingtons, and this included both blue and tan, and liver and tan. I bred both from Gutchcommon stock, and they were proper non-fading terriers too (I have lost count of the fading bi-coloured dogs I have seen over the years, but Gutchcommon stock did not fall into this category).

Liver-coloured specimens were much more plentiful than in the Rillington Bedlingtons, though the addition of Gutchcommon George into Newcombe's lines altered this to a degree. Newcombe's terriers produced more colour variance after George had introduced both Lakeland terrier blood and a combination of Gutchcommon and show breeding (Lady Lena of Eakring). Lena produced blue and tans when mated to George Newcombe's Norman, a dark blue dog that had a coat that reminded me of a Kerry blue terrier rather than a Bedlington. Norman, a dog named after the Leeds United player 'bite your legs' Norman Hunter, was a first-cross Lakeland/Bedlington hybrid and was part of one of Newcombe's pilot experiments to recreate the old Rothbury terrier.

Piggin's Lena was mated to Norman twice. The first blue and tan pup died, so Newcombe persuaded John Piggin to bring Lena back for a repeat litter, and this subsequent union produced not only Newcombe's Venus but also Les Robinson's Amy. Amy was huge, all of nineteen inches to the shoulder but very sound in both type and coat, the latter being non-fading, which in my opinion was in contrast to her sister's poor coat, a fact borne out by later pictures of Venus.

The working Bedlington trend had now reached a period in time when the two prominent and true working strains would branch off and split: one mighty river splitting in two and flowing down different routes. The Gutchcommon line had lost its pioneer Margaret Williamson, Roy Mee had died and John Piggin had been killed in a tragic car crash. This deprived us of a true working dog man who had great affection for not only his beloved Bedlingtons but all working terriers especially the Border terrier, a breed which Piggin admired immensely. Just prior to his tragic and untimely death John Piggin was forging himself quite a reputation as a breeder and aficionado of the gundog breed the Italian Spinone.

There were now few of us left with 'pure' Gutchcommon Bedlingtons, and there was a great temptation to outcross, which I did but I did keep two lines: one hybrid, one pure. Occasionally nice Bedlingtons were brought to The Mad Ratter, Rat Pit Billy and latterly Little Ninja. The pedigrees of some of these were not entirely working strain, containing both Stanolly and Foggyfurze breeding, but my Gutchcommons mated these Bedlingtons, and indeed Rat Pit Billy already had some show breeding from his dam, Rock Star, who was virtually three-quarter-bred Foggyfurze. That union went on to produce Jays Warren Lass, John Denton's bitch who when mated to a show-bred dog produced Staley's Rambo, one of the foremost Bedlington terriers in recent years.

Rambo carried a lot of show breeding but worked like a tiger and forged a hybrid dynasty that is still worked to this very day. It was said Rambo was a throwback, but I actually think the dog was testimony to Staley's skill and perseverance as a proficient trainer of working terriers. I never saw Rambo work in the flesh but I did see videos shown to me by various terrier men, and I agree he was a good working dog. Similarly, Stuart Staley never saw my dogs work, and neither was I ever invited to Stoke to work my dogs, contrary to what may have been written or said elsewhere.

There's no denying that George Newcombe never liked modern show breeding, nor Gutchcommon for that matter, but that didn't stop him using some of it (both in fact) when he wanted to via Lady Lena of Eakring. After judging that ice-bound show at The Furnace Inn at Bedworth, one Terry Reid turned up at the event with a largish blue/black dog that was show bred, and I was very surprised to see that dog had one of the most superb coats I have ever seen on a Bedlington. He asked me what I thought of his dog, and subsequently I sent a copy of the dog's pedigree to George Newcombe who said he would not use or advocate such a show-bred dog. I told Terry Reid his dog had a great coat but was big, in fact too big for earth work, which was fully legal in those far-off days. However, as we all know there have always been big Bedlingtons used primarily as catch dogs above ground or as seizers at the end of a dig on fox or badger when both were legal. Reid's dog had a harsh wiry coat on it, and the dog was aptly called Abbo as its coat resembled the black wiry harshness of the indigenous Australian Aborigines. What happened to Terry or his dog I know not, but I did think at the time – and I still think – that as a non-working-bred dog it could have been a throwback to earlier times, for certainly the vast majority of show dogs don't display the quality of coat that dog did.

The bringing of show and working blood together is not a new practice; its always gone on and show enthusiasts such as Fiona Craig and Ken Bounden are only too familiar with the use of Gutchcommon blood, such unions producing part-bred show, part-bred working-strain dogs of a much improved type. A glance at lots of modern pedigrees reveals how the working strain has been absorbed.

It is interesting to look at the breeding details of Frances Fuller's Plashett Working Bedlingtons, including in parts the breeding of my own Bedlingtons. I never registered either an affix or prefix thinking that at the time it smacked of show orientation which in many ways I suppose it could do, but on the plus side it does identify a family of dogs easily and usually in one word. The pedigrees of Frances's dogs show in parts both work and show strains, and a hallmark of Frances Fuller's dogs is their good coats and ideal height for work. Let's take for example Plashett Blue Marker, a blue and tan dog born in February 1997 and bred by Mrs Fuller. This dog's pedigree interested me straight away when I saw Bridgett of Northlaiths, John Piggin's Bedlington bitch, described as 'liver and white'. Well, that's a new one on me and an obvious mistake for Bridgett was liver. She was lined by the blue dog Sound of Mull who was roughly half working bred from Rillington Raven. A resulting pup from the union produced Gallowdyke Brown Sugar (another Piggin dog), which was mated to Rat Pit Billy in a two-way deal where I used John Piggin's Floyd of Eakring to Bluebell of Strike (another union of note in Fuller's family of Bedlingtons). This was a mutual deal where we both helped each other and no monies changed hands. Within weeks poor John was dead, killed in a fatal car smash and the Bedlington world lost a great stalwart. But his breeding policies lived on.

Newcombe may have voiced his surprise at why Piggin followed this breeding route, and the reason was simply the end result, as in the cliché that goes 'what can't speak can't lie'. The years and the generations that followed clearly proved this to be the case. Gallowdyke Spice of Plashett, the result of the Rat Pit Billy to Gallowdyke Brown Sugar union, was the dam of Plashett Blue Marker, a blue and tan Bedlington. She was paired to the show-bred dog Cullercoats Cracker, a dog you can trace back to Champion Cinnamon of Cullercoats, a dog recorded as sandy and not liver. Cullercoats Cracker also mated Gallowdyke Brown Sugar producing Plashett Blue Laybelle. Frances's Scarlett Emperor of Plashett, otherwise known as Jed, was half John

Holden's Granitor breeding from his sire, the blue dog Granitor Warrior, whose great sire was the very well-known Holden dog, Granitor Joker. Scarlett Emperor of Plashett's dam, the liver bitch Roguehill Rocket, was sired by Westward Blue, a dog I bred from the previously mentioned Floyd of Eakring and Bluebell of Strike. Twice Frances Fuller's stock had benefited from a mutual agreement John Piggin and I had made in the exchange of services of the stud dogs Floyd of Eakring and Rat Pit Billy respectively.

Frances Fuller's dogs prove that a little bit (or lot) of working breeding can do wonders for both type and coat, which answers Newcombe's question why Piggin used the dog he did – the answer is Frances's dogs! Floyd of Eakring was also typical of a show and working-strain collaboration. His sire was the excellent Kentenes Rogue, Roy Mee's Buzzer, a little tyke of only fifteen, albeit sturdy, inches, demonstrating Gutchcommon breeding at its best, and his dam was the show-bred bitch Lucy at Kentoo. John Piggin once said to me simply 'Floyd has been a good dog for me!' and I guess that says it all.

I have worked dogs that have had a combination of working and show breeding and done so very successfully on a wide range of quarry, one of the great unsung being Rock Star, a bitch I knew better as Tina. She came to me via Reg Doyle, a hunter who hailed from Middlesex following a deal I made with Reg involving a Glen of Imaal terrier. I just liked the look of the fifteen-week-old pup so I negotiated a deal and swapped the terriers, and it was only after that I realised I had been so naïve I hadn't even checked the pup's breeding. I need not have worried, however, for what followed was eighteen years of pure pleasure. Tina had already been named – in those days KC application for a new pup's registration often came blank with no name picked – and as Tina Turner was famous at the time she became Rock Star. At around three-quarter show bred and Foggyfurze bred and a quarter Gutchcommon.

I already had a predominantly Gutchcommon-bred bitch of similar age, a puppy bred by Robin Pickard out of his well-known, albeit big and somewhat pale-coated, blue bitch called Bess, aka Little Tyke of Clearwater. Rock Star on the other hand had been bred in Oldham by one Bill Brown whose bitch had allegedly produced ten pups nine of which were bitches! One of these at least was destined to leave her mark after her eighteen-year life.

Tina wed well to rats and rabbits, hunting them with gusto and even going to ground once whilst ferreting and drawing out two live rabbits that were reluctant to bolt. She was a soft terrier on a pre-ban fox but that wasn't to say she wasn't gutsy for often as not Tina could get a fox to bolt and was a delight to work to ground, for she just had a remarkable knack of really irritating her fox holding it at bay and usually bolting it. Digging with her was a pleasure too as you could hear her going berserk baying for England as she sensed you approaching the tube she was in.

She was mated to Bracken (The Mad Ratter) and produced several litters to him, one of her daughters going on to give birth to Stuart Staley's Rambo. Some would say that that mating produced a poor pup that went to Scotland, yet the same pairing produced John Denton's Kizzy, the dam of Rambo, so I don't think it was bad pairing, but it could have been bad entering. It matters little, as Bedlingtons are unique, just like the Border terrier, and their entering can be their undoing. The internet has been a great invention making communication very easy for terrier men, but conversely it has also been a breeding ground for the green-eyed monster, and that playground mentality most of us left in the primary schoolyard.

Bee was a sister to Denton's Kizzy, and she was the dam of Bluebell of Strike who was paired to Floyd of Eakring, and that union produced Lively Lucy, a hard pre-ban foxing bitch, who was as mute as an iron bar but totally reliable on digging. Foxes never got past her – she entered an earth with two things on her mind, find and kill, but that was Luce. Foxes that refused to bolt were engaged underground and killed by this mute bitch.

So, what is the future of the working Bedlington terrier? Certainly its purpose has been curtailed by the current hunting with dogs laws. As I've already said, foxing can only be practised under exempted hunting, and this of course has an effect as the only true test of any working terrier is underground on fox. Throughout its blood-spattered past the terrier has engaged badger and died doing so, has given account of itself on otters, fought other dogs and baited unfortunate creatures that to be honest didn't deserve it (all highly illegal I should add), and hunted in packs pulling down everything from rat to wildcat. Has the breed run its course? The gene pool was always small but now it is hopelessly inbred.

Granitor dog Holly.

The pure-bred Bedlingtons still have their place even in the breeding policies of the hard-liners who only cross-breed their dogs and slate the pure dogs. It is a pity for these dogs are the real outcrosses now; they are the dogs you pair back to when you have any doubts. This is similar to the lurcher breeders when they pair their lurchers back to pure greyhounds. The saying goes: 'if in doubt pair to a greyhound', for of course the racing or former coursing blood is sound and there are so many more of them than there are pure Bedlingtons. Going back to pure can only be good however if the pure dog has overall quality and by that I mean every quality you require in a working terrier. You cannot put quality there in a litter if the parent doesn't have it in the first place!

Is hybridisation the salvation of the Bedlington? Can we call the result a Bedlington? No, it's not the salvation of the *breed*, nor can we possibly call it a Bedlington. What we can do is take away from it a 'splinter' breed and without the constraints of the Kennel Club be free to breed this new type, and give it the greatest accolade you can by giving a new name in the same way the sporting Lucas terrier owners did with their improved working Sealyham types. As we can't call the new type a Bedlington or Rothbury either, I think linty coated terrier would be perfect.

A working standard needs to be established with a breed recording programme (in the same way as show folk have the Kennel Club). We need to preserve our pure dogs, encourage the show folk to breed improved nice-coated dark types, and go away and work them.

The author and terriers ferreting.

Standards must be maintained however, for we don't want them to become mongrels. At a recent BTA event I judged a class, and amongst the entrants there were a couple of unregistered dogs, one allegedly a Bedlington. Clearly it wasn't and neither was it a good outcrossed dog. I remember seeing a similar dog years ago that was bred by a well-known breeder of working Bedlingtons and outcrossed dogs that failed to be one thing or another. In short, a mongrel. With careful breeding the bringing together of several breeds with a Bedlington overtone could eventually produce a type. I feel this direction has great potential and is a project worthy of further consideration.

12 Fit to Work

Working dogs are athletes, performance beings, creatures that need to be fit and sound both physically and mentally if they are to perform well. This was never ever written as a breed manual to discuss dog diseases, the inoculating of pups, the breeding of canines, etc., and I have tried to keep within the perimeters of the book, concentrating on working terriers and running dogs in the field, specifically Bedlingtons and Bedlington lurchers. By the very nature of what they are about, both types of dog (terrier and running dog) are apt to encounter injuries from time to time during the course of their working career. There is no doubt fitness is more important in a running dog than a terrier overall, however make no mistake, terriers running above ground either within a bobbery pack, following hounds or simply bushing rabbits need a great level of fitness, and a running dog because of its working function needs a super fit constitution, and some of these running dogs are easier to get fit than others.

Whippets, for example, are extremely easy to get fit by their very natural willingness to dash around at breakneck speed, fly up hills in top gear and pull like a bull-blooded dog on the leash. Nonetheless any fit dog, at the very peak of its physical training is indeed a sight to behold. A working terrier pre ban was expected to face an adversary with slashing fangs capable of ripping a dog's face to pieces in seconds and needed a certain level of fitness to come to terms with its foe and with indomitable courage kill the fox. A courageous dog is one thing but a fit courageous terrier is another!

However, let's deal with the fitness of our running dogs first, namely the Bedlington lurcher. I am referring here to medium to largish lurchers, that will be greyhound and not whippet bred (though of course I am aware a great number will be whippet bred). I have worked them, and still do to this day, and there is no one who loves the grace, poise and elegance of the whippet more than I do. To my mind the ultimate mini lurcher is the whippet × greyhound and there is only one exception which is more of a specialist longdog.

But, back to our lurcher. This will be a Bedlington × greyhound or possibly greyhound × Bedlington/greyhound (three-quarter-bred greyhound). When it comes to fitness, allow your pup to grow, but don't forget that dogs are wolves and they love to walk and indeed hunt, so it won't be long I promise you before you are out and about with your pup, and whilst the big hounds like the deerhound and wolfhound take longer to mature physically (and incidentally die sooner) whippets and greyhounds are more flexible and thus far superior physically and forgiving mentally.

I am a great advocate of really fit running dogs and terriers too. I love to see a dog oozing pure health and vitality. Smooth dogs (and Bedlingtons and their hybrid running dogs aren't smooth coated) display their physical health beautifully especially black dogs where their muscles literally bulge and glow with vitality, or at least they do when fit. If I could pick a dog breed that epitomises what a dog should be like in the peak of fitness and condition it would be a leggy well-conditioned Stafford, but that doesn't mean to say that a rough-coated lurcher or indeed a Bedlington can't hit those dizzy heights. I have prided myself on getting both rough Bedlington lurchers and working Bedlingtons fit. Pups usually start with loose field work, that is to say they randomly run within the pack at about six months of age with road work increasing steadily from there until they are about nine months old. (There are those who will disagree with that, but that is my opinion and based upon experience.)

By the time they are one year old, the running dogs at least will be catching, and if that first birthday coincides with autumn or winter so much the better, for ideally now begins the first real hunting season. How much road work should you give them? Well, an hour at a good pace is no bother in my experience. Running dogs uphill is also a fantastic way of improving physical appearance but just as it improves a human boxer or martial arts exponent so does it reap benefits for the canine athlete. I guess I really enjoy getting dogs fit just as being a martial arts enthusiast I like to get myself fit training and instructing others. Do you know what? Dogs are no different.

A fit dog is a happy dog and it is also of course healthy and if it is a working dog it will have more than just a chance of being successful. The added benefit is whilst your dog is getting fit so will you!

Working terriers too will need a good level of fitness, though by the very nature of its work where it is expected to pull down its prey it needs a more acute state of physical fitness. By the time the pups are six months old I have them out quite a lot, though the emphasis is on fun, playing, generally enjoying life, and it is this bond that pays fantastic dividends. By the time a running dog is an adult it should find five to ten miles easy, but of course it just depends on how fit you are and how much time you have! A daily road walk of four miles may well be the average, and road work is so important to produce a dog that has a strong overall conformation, tight feet with strong tendons and ligaments, especially when combined with galloping, up hills in particular. Whatever you get out of a dog depends on what you put in, and of course that also means food.

A dog is a wolf, full stop. A pure, raw, carnivore, the archetypal apex predator and a 100 per cent meat eater. That's the way it was intended. Whilst it must conceded that some fruit or vegetable matter may be consumed especially at autumn time, the canid is however essentially a meat eater. Raw warm bloody flesh is the most natural food, this being the way of the wolf through to the African hunting dog, and therefore our Bedlingtons and their kin blood too, in fact all dogs. So why do we feed wheat, that cultivated grass? Now there's a good one! When was the last time you saw a TV documentary or a video on YouTube of a dog taking in the morning air whilst grabbing a paw or two of grass seeds? Far too often these days as in human medical treatment we rely very firmly on synthetic drugs and antibiotics. Nevertheless our natural treatments used successfully for millennia have been largely forgotten and yet they are still available if only folk would ask for them. Modern medicine has somewhat seduced us into feeling this is the only way. The Romans, Anglo Saxons, Vikings and Normans would have used only these natural medicines as would the early English right through medieval times and to the conception of modern medicine with its vaccinations and antibiotics.

Obviously broken bones in the hunting field are only treatable by vets though I have heard of a couple of people who have put plaster casts on their dogs' limbs and set the legs. Of course there is the question of cruelty about this as a dog with a fractured bone whether in limb, jaw or wherever needs professional medical attention. However one would be misled to think that animals don't recover naturally from broken bones, though I am not advocating that in our dogs. Quite the contrary, but to illustrate a point how many of us have caught or shot a rabbit or fox for that matter that looked perfectly healthy before you brought it to book in every way other than it had apparently recovered fully from a fractured limb. Quite probably its body weight would have been normal and it would have had fat laid down around its kidneys. This animal would have recovered without the aid of antibiotics and painkillers.

Rabbits with myxomatosis, a disease similar to bubonic plague, often recover fully and their natural immune system is strengthened tremendously, and also their offspring will be less likely to succumb to this awful malaise.

Enteritis in its many forms claims the lives of lots of newly weaned puppies and ferret kits that have eaten ripe meat and they succumb with alarmingly swift regularity to staphylococci. However, adult dogs and ferrets generally get immunity to such diseases by exposure and rarely succumb to such bacterial infections. Adult dogs sometimes positively relish almost putrid flesh, a legacy from their wolf past. Green tripe, when you could still buy it, must have contained some bacteria yet dogs were drawn to the rank smell it emitted. These animals must have a tremendous quantity of gut flora in a perfect state of balance. I have been looking at natural and herbal medicines and feel this is the way forward in both man and beast; too often today we rely on painkillers and on antibiotics in particular. After an antibiotic is used the next step is to use a probiotic.

Most people can keep a dog fit to work without having to visit the vet but the reader should be aware that bad cuts, suspected broken bones and other serious problems such as suspected poisoning need very prompt veterinary treatment, and there is no substitute for this. I do advocate natural herbal treatments and I do recommend a natural flesh diet for your dog, as it is of course just a domesticated type of wolf.

The wolf, the original dog, is the model of a hunting canine, a natural miracle produced by nature, so why should we as a species try to alter what Mother Nature has created so perfectly?